T0323818

'Aided by lively case studies, the author explores how emotional, relationship and societal pressures may affect sexual confidence, pleasure and functioning. Medical interventions tend to focus purely on the physical issue. Emphasising that sex is about much more than "successful" intercourse, and that sex therapy is about much more than "fixing" the dysfunction, she provides a thorough examination of the different types of sex therapy on offer – from appropriate information-giving to the training and work of a qualified psychosexual therapist.'

Marian O'Connor *is a psychosexual therapist, couple psychoanalytic psychotherapist and former head of MSc in Psychosexual Therapy, Tavistock Relationships*

'Cate's chapter on professionalism addresses the issues of being a psychosexual therapist with a "down to earth" no-nonsense approach, making it very easy to integrate this advice into professional practice. In particular, I was struck by her highlighting the effect that our chosen profession can have on our families, colleagues, personal and professional relationships, and the fantasies and projections they may have about our work. Very sound advice from a very experienced professional, and ideal reading for experienced psychosexual therapists and students alike.'

Jo Coker *is a counselling psychologist and COSRT Professional Standards Manager*

'*Sex Therapy: The Basics* is a courageous attempt to wrestle sex and relationship matters away from the specialist professionals – a decided minority – and to restore them to the vast group of health professionals dealing with them on a day-to-day basis. Her publication treads a fine line between accessibility and the necessary nuances required by this important field. The inclusion of professional issues as well as diversity themes is particularly laudable. As course director of a national training organisation focusing on sex and relationships, I welcome this pioneering work and consider it essential reading.'

Bernd Leygraf *is a consultant psychotherapist and CEO of the Naos Institute*

SEX THERAPY

THE BASICS

Sex Therapy: The Basics offers an introduction to modern sex therapy and is essential reading for anyone working professionally with sexual issues or just interested in sex. This book contains all you need to know to get started, find more information or learn how and when to refer. Current approaches to sex therapy are described, along with detailed interventions and approaches which address an array of sexual issues to bring qualified sex therapists up to date and introduce learners to the essentials. Helping the reader make informed choices about professional development and to find the most appropriate solutions for patients and clients, this book answers all your sex therapy questions.

As well as being essential reading for those considering or interested in sex therapy, this book is a valuable resource for both trainee and experienced therapists, offering contemporary information and advice about assessing and treating a wide range of sexual problems.

Cate Campbell is a sex, relationships and trauma therapist, accredited by the College of Sexual & Relationship Therapists and the British Association for Counselling & Psychotherapy. She has taught for many years, including writing and delivering courses for Relate and the Foundation for Counselling & Relationship Studies and was a visiting lecturer at University College London. She now delivers ad hoc training for organisations like Relate and COSRT. She is also a clinical supervisor and author of *Contemporary Sex Therapy* (2020, Routledge) and *Love and Sex in a New Relationship* (2018, Routledge). She co-presents an informative and entertaining podcast, *The Real Sex Education*.

The Basics

The Basics is a highly successful series of accessible guidebooks which provide an overview of the fundamental principles of a subject area in a jargon-free and undaunting format.

Intended for students approaching a subject for the first time, the books both introduce the essentials of a subject and provide an ideal springboard for further study. With over 50 titles spanning subjects from artificial intelligence (AI) to women's studies, *The Basics* are an ideal starting point for students seeking to understand a subject area.

Each text comes with recommendations for further study and gradually introduces the complexities and nuances within a subject.

SKEPTICISM
JUAN COMESAÑA AND MANUEL COMESAÑA

FILM THEORY (second edition)
KEVIN MCDONALD

SEMIOTICS (fourth edition)
DANIEL CHANDLER

CHOREOGRAPHY
JENNY ROCHE AND STEPHANIE BURRIDGE

ENVIRONMENTAL AND ARCHITECTURAL PSYCHOLOGY
IAN DONALD

NEW RELIGIOUS MOVEMENTS
JOSEPH LAYCOCK

AIR POLLUTION AND CLIMATE CHANGE
JOHN PEARSON AND RICHARD DERWENT

LANGUAGE ACQUISITION
PAUL IBBOTSON

INFANCY
MARC H. BORNSTEIN AND MARTHA E. ARTERBERRY

PHILOSOPHY OF RELIGION
SAMUEL LEBENS

SEX THERAPY

THE BASICS

Cate Campbell

Routledge
Taylor & Francis Group

LONDON AND NEW YORK

Cover image: © Getty Images

First published 2023
by Routledge
4 Park Square, Milton Park, Abingdon, Oxon OX14 4RN

and by Routledge
605 Third Avenue, New York, NY 10158

Routledge is an imprint of the Taylor & Francis Group, an informa business

British Library Cataloguing-in-Publication Data
A catalogue record for this book is available from the British Library

Library of Congress Cataloging-in-Publication Data
Names: Campbell, Cate (Relationship therapist), author.
Title: Sex therapy : the basics / Cate Campbell.
Description: Abingdon, Oxon ; New York, NY : Routledge, 2023. |
Includes bibliographical references and index. |
Identifiers: LCCN 2022013145 (print) | LCCN 2022013146 (ebook) |
ISBN 9781032208732 (hbk) | ISBN 9781032208718 (pbk) |
ISBN 9781003265641 (ebk)
Subjects: LCSH: Sex therapy.
Classification: LCC RC557 .C36 2023 (print) | LCC RC557 (ebook) |
DDC 616.85/83--dc23/eng/20220629
LC record available at https://lccn.loc.gov/2022013145
LC ebook record available at https://lccn.loc.gov/2022013146

ISBN: 978-1-032-20873-2 (hbk)
ISBN: 978-1-032-20871-8 (pbk)
ISBN: 978-1-003-26564-1 (ebk)

DOI: 10.4324/9781003265641

Typeset in Bembo
by Taylor & Francis Books

CONTENTS

ACKNOWLEDGEMENTS

I'm deeply grateful for the assistance of Jo Coker, COSRT professional standards manager, plus Sara White and the nurses of Prostate Cancer UK. Special thanks also to Meg-John Barker for her support and advice with Chapter 4.

INTRODUCTION

Sexual problems are not necessarily a reflection of a relationship's quality. They may, however, affect this if the couple are unable to manage any resulting anxiety, shame or distress. Thus, the 'problem' may have been easily fixed, but its consequences remain. Accordingly, couples seeking sex therapy have often already been down a medical or couple counselling route by the time they present. Usually, neither has offered a complete solution, though they may both have provided some help. Sex therapy is able to offer a biopsychosocial approach by bringing together all the influences on the problem and formulating a way forward.

> A *biopsychosocial approach* is interested in the connections between biological, psychological and social aspects of an issue, including how they interact and influence it, rather than just looking through a medical lens.

Some sex therapists have a medical qualification, as well as training in sex and relationship therapy, and are able to offer a comprehensive approach. It's an advantage if they're able to examine their patients, order investigations, refer and prescribe. However, sex therapists can suggest their clients request medical interventions, such as a vaginal examination, blood tests for hormone levels or specialist referral. Indeed, it could be considered unethical for a therapist to withhold such advice if this may be helpful. Moreover, a non-medical sex therapist may be more likely to see couples rather than just the

DOI: 10.4324/9781003265641-1

individual who identifies with a problem. This helps the therapist to recognise and resolve any issues partners have too, and also to appreciate how they each trigger the other's anxiety and how their relationship dynamic serves to maintain their problems.

That's obviously not to say that individuals don't have sexual problems. Of course, they do and these often considerably predate a couple's issues. Seeking help early offers the opportunity to treat or improve what's happening before anxiety has the chance to grow and contaminate every sexual encounter. An individual may, for instance, receive medical treatment for a tight foreskin causing sexual pain. Someone may be given exercises to manage **vaginismus**, erectile difficulty or early ejaculation. Or they may simply receive information which improves their understanding about what's happening and, through discussion, changes unhelpful thinking and beliefs which are impacting or causing their issues.

As we'll see in Chapter 1, which explores what sex therapy is all about, there's a continuum involving all kinds of practitioners, from a nurse who offers advice to patients post-surgery, to the counsellor discussing sexual or identity issues, to the psychosexual therapist with advanced skills who works with clinical sexual dysfunctions, psychosocial and relationship issues and maybe other specialisms such as sexual trauma, often using a variety of modalities. The chapter goes on to describe the PLISSIT Model, a four-stage progression which sets out the tasks required at each stage of the continuum. The types of training available for each stage are described, including entry routes and progression, explaining how this has broadened considerably in recent years as a reaction to the medicalisation of sexual problems. There is a simple look at couple counselling, which may be required or incorporated into some of the trainings. So, as well as being helpful to those considering a career in sex therapy or beginning their psychosexual therapy training, this book will offer advice to anyone interested in improving their knowledge and skills about sexual matters.

> The *medicalisation* of sexual 'problems' has meant they've been explored from a clinical perspective which seeks medical solutions. This implies having no problems is 'normal', whereas the complexity of sex and relationships means that negotiating and experimenting with what works is actually most people's experience.

Chapter 2 contains description of the kinds of sexual problems which might be encountered by sex therapists, including 'dysfunctions' listed in the US *Diagnostic & Statistical Manual-5* (DSM). The chapter goes on to look at other issues which may exacerbate or lead to sexual dysfunctions, such as body image, sex throughout the life span and the way we think. The suggestions offered here to improve the problems described would be augmented with treatments found elsewhere in the book, especially those described in Chapter 3, which explores solutions. Different approaches to sex therapy are discussed, beginning with the core Cognitive Behaviour Therapy (CBT) model. The entire process is explained, including discussion of assessment, sensate focus and other interventions, managing blocks and ending. Other approaches include the medical model, systemic therapy, feminist approaches, parts therapies and psychodynamic therapies, including Imago and Transactional Analysis. A section on attachment includes both mentalizing and Emotionally Focused Therapy.

Exploration of different forms of sexuality and gender identity is the focus of Chapter 4, from straight cis identity to gay, bisexual and trans identities, what the enactment of masculinity and femininity means to people and how polyamory and asexuality may affect couple relationships. There's a look at how these identities developed and whether it's helpful to apply labels. Support for coming out is discussed, as well as therapist self-disclosure and attitudes. Throughout, the chapter considers what might be needed in therapy.

Throughout the book, 'woman' and 'man' are used to refer to both cisgender and trans men and women. The term LGBT+ (Lesbian, Gay, Bisexual, Trans and other non-binary or different identities) has been replaced throughout by GSRD which stands for Gender, Sexual and Relationship Diverse/Diversity. This is now felt to better represent the vast range of gender and sexual identities and also to be inclusive of relationship diversity; for example, polyamory. Of course, everyone – however they identify – has gender, sexual and relationship diversity. It's used here to describe people who are marginalised in relation to their GSRD.

Chapter 5, 'Specialist areas', looks at issues not yet covered which don't necessarily fit neatly into other sections. The sections provide necessary rudimentary information for therapists so they have a resource and fundamental awareness of the subjects, how to find further information and when to refer. The likelihood of meeting the issues is addressed, alongside the therapist's potential stance. Sexual dependency is covered, including the effects of extreme pornography use and use of anabolic steroids. Paraphilias and offending are also mentioned. A section on sexually transmitted and genital infections includes bacterial, viral and yeast infections, parasites and HIV. A part exploring relational issues includes tantric sex, sex toys, sexomnia fantasy and kink. In a section on trauma, there's information about female genital mutilation (FGM), shame, safeguarding, talking to children about sex, technology and affairs. A discussion of neurodiversity closes the chapter, with a look at attention deficit disorder and autistic spectrum disorder.

Professionalism and the image of sex therapists is discussed in Chapter 6, including how to manage this along with other relevant areas such as social media use, career development, supervision, therapist safety and self-care. A section on ethics includes topics such as confidentiality, consent and delivering therapy online.

The book ends with a bibliography and a glossary of terms which may be unfamiliar and are printed bold in the book. Some potentially unfamiliar terms which go on to be explained in the text are italicised.

It's very much hoped that this introduction to sex therapy will be helpful, whether you're thinking of sex therapy as a career, already working or training as a sex therapist, engaged in related work or just interested.

WHAT IS SEX THERAPY?

At its most basic, sex therapy could be described as any information, exploration, intervention, behaviour, conversation or way of thinking which improves sexual functioning, image or identity. On this basis, sex therapy can happen accidentally, say, when someone reads a helpful article, has an enlightening conversation or even just loses a few pounds and feels more body confident. Many individuals and couples also make deliberate attempts to change their sexual feelings, response or repertoire, often with the help of media information, which can be extremely useful or make matters worse. Sometimes an over-dramatic article or TV programme can provoke unnecessary worry. Indeed, the more we're bombarded with sexual content, the harder it can be to work out what's okay, what needs to be addressed and what is just rubbish.

Lurking in the back of the mind of people with sexual problems may be the idea that they can consult a sex therapist if their situation becomes dire enough. So by the time many people present, they have accumulated considerable feelings of guilt and hopelessness, fuelled by impressions of what others are achieving sexually. Indeed, one of the reasons sexual problems often go unaddressed for so long is the shame associated with what's seen as sexual failure and a fear that sex therapy will be even more shaming. Part of this is a result of sex therapy being a bit of a mystery, portrayed as either comical or a little bit threatening. Because they often don't know what to expect, many couples fear they'll be required to have sex in the therapist's consulting room or made to feel somehow responsible or inadequate. They may not see sex therapists as health professionals like any other, or may feel there is stigma attached to seeing one. They may not even know how to find one.

DOI: 10.4324/9781003265641-2

The first port of call for many people is not a qualified sex therapist, but another health professional who is readily accessible, such as their GP, health visitor or youth worker. It's consequently common for health practitioners to find themselves delivering some form of sex therapy unintentionally. Even when this is simply a matter of signposting to an appropriate resource, they need the knowledge to do this. Talking about sex also requires them to be able to have conversations in a containing and open way, so that neither they nor their patients feel embarrassed or fearful of offending. Those who provide sexual information may find themselves doing so simply because they're the only person on hand to approach for advice in an out-patient clinic or because it's procedure to hand out leaflets about sex or fertility. It's understandable that some health providers working in contexts with no evident sexual affinity feel ill-equipped or uncomfortable with this role, while those working in other contexts may see sexual information giving or advice as an obvious part of their job. The midwife explaining future contraception or what to expect following genital tears in childbirth, family planning centre staff being quizzed about the effects of contraceptives on sexual functioning and sexual health or screening clinics providing advice about safer sex all provide a gateway for service users to seek more. Information may be sought or offered in many other settings too, such as in general practice, religious ministries, schools, colleges and youth clubs, support organisations and social work. From these starting places there is a continuum all the way through different degrees of expertise, experience and educational attainment towards the fully qualified sex therapist. Understandably, this may lead accidental practitioners to look for ways to deepen their knowledge and skills.

In the USA, where sex education is seen as a career in its own right, or identified practitioners may have had additional training to offer sex education, it's potentially a little easier to be offered training and for the public to identify and access the support they need. For instance, someone seeking advice about sexual functioning following prostate surgery might be automatically referred to, or approached by, a sex educator. In the UK this role could be provided by anyone from a health-care assistant with no training at all to a fully qualified sex therapist.

CASE STUDY 1: OMAR

Omar, who was in his early fifties, went to see his GP due to abdominal pain and needing to get up for a wee more often at night. The GP performed a rectal examination which suggested Omar had a slightly enlarged prostate. An initial urine specimen didn't show any abnormalities, but a blood test to check prostate specific antigen (PSA) levels showed they were slightly raised. The GP called Omar to explain that this could be due to a prostate condition, so he was going to refer him to a urologist.

Omar panicked. That evening he told his husband Jim how worried he was. He thought the urologist may say that he needed surgery to remove his prostate, which Omar had heard can cause erectile difficulties. Also, because he enjoyed anal sex and prostate stimulation, he convinced himself that his sex life was over. Jim tried to comfort him and suggested that he call the surgery the next day.

The receptionist he spoke to asked a nurse to call him back. She e-mailed him a couple of leaflets and suggested that he call a specialist nurse at Prostate Cancer UK (0800 074 8383) or access their sexual support service online (https://prostatecanceruk.org/get-support/sexual-support), though she explained that it was much too soon to assume he had cancer. The specialist nurse also reassured him about this and explained the different conditions that can cause an enlarged prostate, including just getting older. She asked him if he'd had any prostate stimulation or anal sex before the PSA blood test. When she heard that he had, she explained that this can be responsible for raised PSA levels and that he could ask the GP to repeat the test, abstaining from prostate stimulation for a few days beforehand. She told him that even if he did need surgery, he could be referred to an ED clinic afterwards, and that surgeons didn't rush to treat prostate problems but would often wait to see what developed.

The leaflets reinforced what the nurse had said and Omar felt less worried. A repeat PSA test produced normal results, and the urologist who examined him did not think his prostate was significantly enlarged anyway. Omar noticed that his abdominal pain and need to wee had gone away, which the urologist thought might have been due to the resolution of an infection, dietary or lifestyle changes. He explained that Omar could request further PSA tests every year. Both Omar and Jim felt reassured and much more prepared should either of them develop a prostate problem in the future.

PLISSIT MODEL

In the 1970s the variation in training led US psychologist Jack Annon to develop The PLISSIT Model, which attempts to categorise the level of intervention necessary for different outcomes. Standing for **P**ermission, **L**imited **I**nformation, **S**pecific **S**uggestions and **I**ntensive **T**reatment, the model provides boundaries and objectives at each of its four stages.

PERMISSION SEEKING

Permission seeking is actually crucial to each stage of the process, to prevent practitioners from making assumptions about what is required. For instance, a nurse might ask a patient if they would be interested in a leaflet about post-surgery sex rather than simply handing it to them. Similarly, rather than just telling a patient they will examine them, and asking them to undress, a doctor would first enquire whether this would be okay. In modern PLISSIT delivery, practitioners also check how the service user is feeling about what's being delivered, including finding out whether they want to continue with the process if that's relevant. Permission also requires practitioners to be available for questions and conversations, and to be able to assess which sources of help would be most appropriate for the individual or couple. Where possible, they should also follow up how helpful their intervention turned out to be, as a way of informing future service provision as well as assisting the current patient further.

LIMITED INFORMATION

Limited Information and the knowledge that it's acceptable to discuss sex may be all that some people need. However, this may change so that more becomes necessary and others may need immediate referral to someone more experienced. In medical settings this may be a specialist, such as a gynaecologist, urologist, physiotherapist, dermatologist or psychiatrist.

Doctors who have qualified as sex therapists are obviously able to offer physical examinations to their patients, but more often doctors and sex therapists work in tandem to find solutions which combine medical intervention alongside mental health support. Some hospital departments have sex therapy teams where patients automatically see a doctor and a psychosexual therapist if they present with a physical sexual problem, such as painful sex, or a physical issue or treatment which may affect sexual function, such as some cancers, gynaecological or prostate problems. Other hospitals have sex therapists available who accept referrals from all departments, but in many the onus remains on the clinicians to provide sexual health information. Through experience, some of these practitioners become able to offer specific suggestions about ways to manage or improve sexual wellbeing, though they are more likely to work with individual patients than to see them with their partners in a more defined sex therapy process.

In mental health settings, too, practitioners may find themselves discussing sex and relationships, and may be able to offer helpful conversations. However, good-enough sex therapy is not just about sex positivity, common sense or restoring an ability to have intercourse. Sex means different things to different people at different times, so what they need from sex therapy may be much more than just a 'diagnosis' and a straightforward 'treatment'. For example, having established that someone has erectile difficulties (ED), a potential solution may appear to be prescription of a drug like Viagra. But Viagra won't work if the patient has no desire, does not receive sufficient sexual stimulation, is very anxious, feels guilty or doesn't actually want to have sex. All of these may need to be addressed, along with other factors such as the effect on their relationship, each partner's beliefs about how sex should be and what's happening, and ways their previous life and sexual experiences influence the way they see what's happened.

Treatment is not just a matter of offering a solution and hoping it works. Sex therapy is about empowering the individual or couple to ultimately feel in control of their sexual feelings and behaviour. If we're honest, many of us feel nothing of the sort. We reach for ideas about how sex should be and then just strive to achieve them. But sex is so personal, and special to each one of us, that broad brush ways of approaching it are unlikely to be truly helpful. One person's route to ecstasy is likely to be another's complete turnoff.

SPECIFIC SUGGESTIONS

Increasing medicalisation of sexual problems has led to more interest in holistic approaches and the involvement of partners where possible to explore the effect of sexual problems on the whole relationship. Treatment approaches work best when they are collaborative rather than imposed by an expert professional, so specific suggestions may actually come from the service users themselves. This doesn't mean that the therapist has no ideas, but that it's more helpful to enable people to find their own solutions, albeit supported by suggestions and advice. Often, therapy encourages a different way of seeing the problem which either makes it seem less troublesome or allows solutions to emerge. Medical interventions alone can't address the ways people think which keep their problems going or may even have caused them in the first place. A Viagra prescription is also worthless if it offends someone's sense of masculinity. Many men genuinely believe that a 'need' for help with their erections signals a fundamental flaw in themselves. Many would rather dodge the flaw showing up by avoiding sex than take medication. Similarly, some partners believe that a problem wouldn't exist if they were attractive enough, which can also lead to sexual avoidance in both partners. A sex therapist could offer detailed information about the incidence of erection difficulties and the way that anxiety then causes recurrence. Techniques to manage anxiety and the development of less rigid thinking in both partners would help them to feel more in control. Most people also benefit from adopting a less **phallocentric** attitude to sex, whereby they become less concerned with the performance of the penis and intercourse, and more interested in a relaxed and enjoyable sexual experience. Perhaps surprisingly, trying *not* to focus on outcomes like erection and orgasm makes it much more likely that they will happen.

Even experienced relationship therapists sometimes continue to promote unhelpful ways of thinking about sex or feel awkward discussing it. Couple counsellors are not always trained to talk about sex or are comfortable doing so, which means some refer immediately for medical or psychosexual assessment when a sexual issue is mentioned. On the other hand, some are overconfident about their ability to discuss sex when they don't actually have the knowledge or training to do so, often assuming that sex therapy is just about sex positivity. In fact, though a sex positive attitude is permission giving, there also needs to be some curiosity about sexual behaviour rather than just blanket acceptance. Some people will tell the therapist what they think is expected of them or what they think will avoid censure. In fact, a curious attitude whereby the therapist doesn't just accept what they're told, or make assumptions about what they've understood, is ultimately considerably less judgemental than presuming. Some relationship therapists who aren't fully trained as sex therapists are nonetheless very skilled at this. For instance, they may have considerable experience in working with issues like sexual identity, trauma or mismatched libido, whilst referring to a more qualified practitioner for clinical issues involving sexual functioning, such as problems with orgasm, sexual pain and arousal.

Because help is provided on such a wide continuum, at the most basic information giving/seeking level, training may simply involve word of mouth protocols or brief in-house training sessions. Practitioners may be seconded or may need to seek their own additional training, which may be offered as Continuous Professional Development by their employer or by organisations such as the College of Sexual & Relationship Therapists (COSRT), Relate or other training providers. Some of these also offer courses in ways to talk about sex and how to recognise and refer sexual dysfunctions. These may assist couple counsellors as well as clinical practitioners wishing to expand their knowledge and skills without completing a full sex therapy training.

INTENSIVE TREATMENT

In the UK, practitioners qualified in providing intensive treatment for sexual problems are often known as psychosexual therapists, and the treatment they provide is psychosexual therapy (PST). Usually trained in both relationship therapy and treatment for specific sexual problems, they may use a wide range of interventions which address behavioural issues, relationship difficulties and any mental health consequences. As explained above, for instance, a single episode of erectile difficulty may cause so much anxiety that losing an erection becomes almost inevitable whenever the person attempts partnered sex. The partner may feel unattractive and unloved as a result, with neither of the couple feeling confident about initiating sex, which is consequently avoided, with desire becoming suppressed and eventually lost altogether. By the time the couple present for help, there may be a number of complex relationship issues to unpick in addition to the (now) two sexual problems of ED and loss of desire.

Sex therapists also need to be able to refer to other practitioners if necessary. In this case, just consulting the GP may reassure the couple if tests show there is no organic cause. But this won't just switch back on their lost desire. Restoring the couple's confidence and trust in one another, and developing behaviours which comfortably facilitate intimacy, will require experimentation and containment.

In addition to needing multiple skills and knowledge, including an understanding of sexual anatomy and physiology, it's clear that sex therapists need to be able to work with relationship dynamics and the way each partner's history influences their response to the other, as well as their overall mental health. Generalised couple problems can obviously lead to sexual problems, however, and the way the couple approach sexual problems also relates to the way they 'do' their relationship.

This is incredibly rewarding work, requiring multiple nuanced skills. Just as sex therapy ranges from gentle information and signposting all the way through to intensive treatment, training to become a sex therapist also exists on a continuum. As more health practitioners become aware of their role in offering or beginning a healing process for their patients or clients, training providers have responded with foundation courses which enhance the work of non-therapist practitioners. This equips and enables those who wish to offer a more targeted and effective service to be able to answer questions, offer advice and make appropriate referrals, both to NHS and private providers. Counselling and psychotherapy training also does not always include ways to discuss sex, self-image, identity and relationships though these are fundamental to many people's mental health issues.

CASE STUDY 2: CARLA AND HANS

Carla and Hans had both spoken to their GP about sexual problems during the year before they started looking for sex therapy. Carla, 47, was bothered by night sweats, brain fog, low mood, irregular heavy periods and a decline in libido. The GP thought she was peri-menopausal and referred her to a menopause clinic which pre-scribed hormone replacement therapy (HRT) and mentioned sex therapy as part of an holistic approach to her issues. Hans, 49, consulted the GP around the same time as he was having difficulty ejaculating during partnered sex. The GP ran some blood tests which seemed to rule out organic causes, and wondered if Hans was anxious. She also mentioned sex therapy.

Initially, neither of the couple seriously considered this, assum-ing they could resolve things by themselves. Gradually, though, they found they were avoiding all forms of touch and realised that it had been ten months since there was any sexual contact between them. It was Carla who started looking for help and then told Hans, wondering if he would be annoyed. He was actually relieved.

During history taking, the sex therapist established that Carla no longer felt like a sexual being. Being hot and sweaty so much, having put on some weight, and constantly comparing herself with her beautiful and energetic teenage daughters, Carla just didn't feel sexy. The therapist also learned that Hans' problem with ejaculating had begun during Carla's pregnancies. He hadn't made the con-nection, but it seemed he felt ashamed of his wish to make love to her when he believed she didn't really want to.

In therapy, the couple experimented with sensate focus exercises which allowed them to reconnect through touch. Carla found new ways of recognising her sexuality and they both benefited from consent exercises which helped Hans in particular to believe that Carla did find him attractive and wanted to make love. This also allowed them to enjoy intimacy and touch without feeling obliged to progress to intercourse. In fact, they extended their sexual repertoire considerably. Carla was able to make the most of the times she felt desire and Hans no longer had difficulty climaxing.

TRAINING

While adhering to the COSRT criteria for courses, there is none-theless a considerable difference in the types of training available to become a qualified psychosexual therapist, equipped to manage the psychological, emotional, social and physical challenges of sexual problems. Some courses focus more on talking therapies, and exploration of sexual identity, for instance, while others are more clinically directed. Some approaches encourage the use of home-work and behavioural experimentation, while others are more directed towards improving the relationship and each partner's sexual barriers so that sex becomes more possible. Though it isn't necessary to attend a foundation course before training as a sex therapist, some counselling skills are helpful and, unless relationship therapy is an explicit part of the sex therapy training, couple counselling experience will be needed. A number of courses cover the basics of relationship dynamics, attachment and simple inter-ventions, with a requirement for at least 50 hours of practical experience alongside.

> The New Relationship Energy experienced during the honeymoon period is a result of hormones which cause us to feel obsessed with our new partner, obscuring awareness of their faults and boosting libido. This is nature's way of making us bond, and only lasts from six months to three years. Loss of New Relationship Energy can be accelerated by commitment behaviours, such as moving in together or becoming pregnant.

WHO NEEDS SEX THERAPY?

Despite often having only vague ideas about what relationship and sex therapy involve, more couples are seeking help. This may be due to the greater awareness of health professionals or the vastly reduced stigma associated with therapy. In the UK many social changes have resulted in different relationship and sexual expecta-tions. From the 1960s, the combination of reliable contraception, more liberal divorce legislation, legalisation of homosexuality, higher wages and research into sexual functioning have allowed couples to make more choices about their relationships. Before this, many couples married due to accidental pregnancy and put up with unhappy relationships. Now, many couples not only expect happy relationships but assume there's something badly wrong if this happiness doesn't happen 'naturally' and without effort. This includes the idea that sexual compatibility is established in the early part of the relationship – the honeymoon period, also discussed on pages 48–49 – and will endure. Though couples often find ways to improve their relationship, they can't recapture this honeymoon period, though they often present for sex therapy with the aim of doing so. Indeed, increased openness about sex has led to much more dissatisfaction, with many people feeling entitled to fulfil all their erotic desires with their partner. The problem with this is that both partners are unlikely to share exactly the same hopes and expectations, meaning fulfilment of one may require the other to sublimate their own wishes or agree to behaviours they dislike. Partners' desire also fluctuates depending on their circumstances, so it's natural to go through times when sex is rare. This is often just due to exhaustion and lack of opportunity, with some couples so busy they rarely meet, let alone have time for sex. Yet, instead of blaming their circumstances, partners blame one another and assume sexual incompatibility.

The expectation of sexual compatibility and the gratification of needs is another relatively recent social change which has increased the pressure on couples despite superficially offering greater opportunities for mutuality, connection and sexual pleasure. Rather than taking responsibility for their own sexual experience, many partners expect the other to do this, creating an unnecessary preoccupation with performance and outcomes which can escalate anxiety. Particularly in straight relationships, men may become fixated on getting and keeping an erection and 'making' their partners 'achieve' an orgasm, leaving little room for actual desire, eroticism, relaxation and pleasure. Partners, meanwhile, may strive to orgasm in order to please, as this seems so important. Indeed, some couples believe there is something wrong with the relationship if all these outcomes aren't met, and that the relationship has failed. Helping couples to rediscover the delight of an exploratory sexual journey, rather than just the delivery of sexual destinations, is a basic task in sex therapy.

Sex and relationship issues are inevitably exacerbated, or even caused, by inability to communicate effectively, usually due to assumptions about what the other means or wants which are never explored. The therapist's modelling of a curious, respectful approach, where listening and checking is used effectively to help each partner feel heard, is a major therapeutic tool by itself. Many partners are so afraid of getting something wrong that they feel they must 'know' what the other partner thinks and needs without ever asking. Indeed, some partners are so afraid of discussing needs that they end up doing so with someone else, often resulting in an emotional or sexual affair. Couples frequently seek therapy in the aftermath of affairs, when sex can sometimes be passionate and bonding, only to stall as the couple begin to negotiate their way through the hurt. The expectation that they can return to 'normal' is unrealistic, especially as the experience of guilt, blame and pain change who we are and how we respond. Though some affairs are conducted as a way of ending a relationship, many couples want to continue and can be helped to discover how to be vulnerable, open and available in ways that may not have been possible before (see also pages 159–160).

When relationships have ended badly, new partners sometimes seek therapy to try to avoid the problems of the past. Indeed, a new relationship is often the impetus for someone to deal with a longstanding sexual problem. There may also be issues of trust when a partner has been badly hurt previously, and not just because of affairs. While pornography can positively enhance partnered and solo sex for many people, recent ease of access to online pornography can sometimes promote unrealistic expectations of sex and make intimate partnered sex seem less exciting, leaving partners feeling inadequate and unloved. Poor experiences of coming out, a difficult journey to transition, abuse, asexuality or guilt about ending a relationship are just a handful of ways new relationships can be affected by past difficulties.

Not all couples seeking relationship or sex therapy actually want to change either. Sometimes, they bring one another to therapy as a way of blaming, shaming and denying their own responsibility. When the other partner is enthusiastic about the therapy process, they may lose interest or intensify the blame, sometimes targeting the therapist as well as their partner.

Sometimes couples need permission to end their relationship. Framing a relationship which has allowed the personal growth and development of each partner as successful can allow couples to separate without feeling they've failed. Other couples have grown so close that sex is impossible, provoking a kind of incest taboo as they now feel like relatives. Though they may deeply love each other, they no longer feel sexual together. There are ways of regaining a spark, but many couples anticipate an inferno and may not feel they should settle for less.

Couples may be affected by illness which has impacted their capacity for sex. As well as needing help with the mechanics of sex when impacted by physical challenges, some couples discover mental health problems which can affect their relationship in unexpected ways. Some may lose interest in sex altogether while others may seek multiple sexual experiences, acquire new sexual interests or make inappropriate sexual remarks. Often, caring for someone with a health problem can make a partner feel more like a nurse than a lover, so that the couple need help to make practical changes to their everyday lives and introduce more romance.

As well as developing a capacity to manage relationship distress, sex therapists need to be able to recognise, tolerate and assess when a couple's conflict has escalated to dangerous levels. Safeguarding issues are commonplace in work with couples, where there is often a power imbalance or control which skews the relationship to the extent that sex therapy cannot be considered consensual. Clues can be subtle. For instance, it's understandable to feel sympathy for a partner who says they feel unloved because sex is a rare part of the relationship. However, it needs to be ascertained what is meant by both 'sex' and 'rare'. Sometimes a partner's extreme demands for sexual availability are only one of many requirements which serve to control the other, who may be afraid to reveal the extent of this control or unaware of how unusual it is. In such cases, part of the therapist's role is determining how to proceed safely or end the therapy in a way that supports each partner without increasing risk.

The academic requirements for sex therapy training vary too, with some courses having considerable experiential content where students examine how their own experience and attitudes will affect this work. This is important for all sex therapy practitioners, but some courses also require advanced evidence of academic ability, involving considerably more reading and essay writing. At the moment, courses leading to a recognised sex therapy qualification range from Level 5, which is equivalent to the second year of a degree, to Level 7 which would lead to a master's degree or Postgraduate Diploma at master's level. Candidates awarded a master's degree normally undertake some sort of research. Some even go on afterwards to study for a Professional Doctorate or PhD.

ADDITIONAL SKILLS

Whatever level is studied, the comprehensive training is usually only the beginning of the extensive skills that sex therapists develop during their careers as they continuously add to their knowledge and abilities, sometimes introducing other modalities which may be helpful, such as:

- **EMDR** to treat sexual trauma
- **Mentalization**, which can help people more effectively consider their own and others' thinking and acceptance of personal responsibility
- Systemic therapies to further explore the effects of familial and cultural attitudes or gender, sexual and relationship diversity
- And **parts therapies** which explore an individual's competing internal interests.

Other specialist training could be related to, say, the psychosexual consequences of infertility, sexual dependency or sexual offending. Some sex therapists specialise in working with particular sexual problems, such as sexual pain, though most have received a generic training and can work with almost any sexual problems. Practitioners in the NHS are more likely to work with individuals than couples, and those with a separate relationship therapy qualification are more likely to have experience working with a couple's general issues as well as sexual ones.

PROFESSIONAL BODIES

Many sex therapists belong to COSRT, a professional body with different categories of membership. Affiliates are members with an interest in sex therapy but no relevant role, while Professional Associates are those working in allied roles, such as relationship therapists and health-care professionals. Professional Associates benefit from access to the COSRT newsletter and the *Journal of Sexual and Relationship Therapy*, as well as some training discounts. Those undertaking COSRT professional qualification accredited training join as student members, with all the benefits of Professional Associates, plus access to COSRT's Practice Guidelines. They're also placed on a register of sex therapy students so that members of the public are able to check they're genuinely in training.

On qualification, they're able to apply to join the COSRT Register of Psychosexual and Relationship Therapists, which requires them to follow COSRT's guidelines on practice, professional conduct and ongoing professional development. Accreditation gives them access to professional listings, training and other academic discounts and may improve employment opportunities, although many sex therapists work in private practice. To apply for COSRT accreditation, applicants must have three years of postgraduate experience as a psychosexual therapist and have been COSRT registered for at least a year. They must also fulfil other requirements including 150 hours of supervised practice and 80 hours of personal therapy. Some go on to train as supervisors, who may also be COSRT registered and can seek accreditation as supervisors. Those with master's degrees, in particular, may progress to become lecturers on training courses themselves, often acquiring a teaching qualification.

Depending on all their training and qualifications, sex therapists may be registered with other professional bodies as well, such as the UK Council for Psychotherapy (UKCP), the British Association for Counselling and Psychotherapy (BACP), the Association for the Treatment of Sexual Addiction and Compulsivity (ATSAC), the British Infertility Counselling Association (BICA), Association of Christian Counsellors (ACC) and Pink Therapy. Further information about the professional aspects of sex therapy can be found in Chapter 6.

CHAPTER SUMMARY

- Aspects of sex therapy exist on a continuum from signposting support to providing complex psychological and clinical treatment.

- Jack Annon's PLISSIT Model organises this continuum in practical terms for use by health care professionals.
- Qualified sex therapists in the UK have had a comprehensive training and are often trained as relationship therapists too.

FURTHER READING

Maier, T. (2013) *Masters of Sex: The Life and Times of William Masters and Virginia Johnson, the Couple Who Taught America How to Love*, New York: Basic Books.

Perel, E. (2005) *Mating in Captivity: Unlocking Erotic Intelligence*, London: Hodder & Stoughton.

Taylor, B. & David, S. (2007) The Extended PLISSIT Model for addressing the sexual wellbeing of individuals with an acquired disability or chronic illness. *Sexuality & Disability*, 25, 135–139.

RESOURCES

COSRT accredited sex therapy courses: www.cosrt.org.uk/accredited-professional-courses/.

BIBLIOGRAPHY

Annon, J.S. (1976) The PLISSIT Model: A proposed conceptual scheme for the behavioral treatment of sexual problems. *Journal of Sex Education and Therapy*, 2(1), 1–15.

PROBLEMS

2

There is a vast range of sexual problems which are addressed by sex therapists, many of which are social or relational in nature. These are classified among other mental health issues by both the World Health Organization's *International Statistical Classification of Diseases and Related Health Problems* (ICD) and the *Diagnostic & Statistical Manual* (DSM), compiled by the American Psychiatric Association (APA). The ICD, now in its tenth edition, has existed for more than a century and aims to improve clarity about conditions internationally. The DSM, meanwhile, has been used since 1952 and essentially applies to the USA. Throughout its existence, the DSM has reflected social attitudes to mental health conditions, and particularly sexual issues. The range of mental health conditions has burgeoned, with only 60 included in DSM-I and more than 300 appearing in the latest edition, DSM-5.

These manuals provide codes for the payment of health insurance and are also a resource for practitioners. In the UK many courses teach sex therapy using the classifications in the DSM because they are more specific than those in the ICD. Some sex therapy courses have historically been quite rigid about training their students only to work with conditions clinically described in the DSM, considering that more general issues, relating to sexual communication for instance, could be addressed by couple counsellors. However, though the work of sex therapists has now broadened out considerably from the original clinical remit, it's important to be familiar with DSM 'sexual dysfunctions'. These have a physical effect which interferes with sexual functioning and

DOI: 10.4324/9781003265641-3

broadly include arousal and desire disorders, pain/sensation disorders and issues with orgasm and ejaculation. Conditions caused by drugs or substances and other clinical problems which don't fit easily into another category are also addressed in the DSM. To qualify as a dysfunction, they must cause distress and have existed continuously for at least six months.

AROUSAL AND DESIRE DISORDERS

Sexual arousal is simply an involuntary bodily response to mental or physical stimulation. Desire is much more complex and hard to define. Could a wish to have sex even though you don't feel like it be seen as desire? Or is desire just a willingness to be sexual? Is it something to do with attraction towards someone? Or does it have to be accompanied by arousal? The reality is that desire isn't something that can be turned on and off at will, though it can certainly be supressed. We need appropriate circumstances to feel desire, and they're often not there. Many couples who complain of sexual infrequency and loss of desire find it returns the moment they step off the plane at their holiday destination. Work, parenting, domestic chores and familiarity don't promote desire. Indeed, there's evidence that sexual behaviour decreased for many couples locked down together during the pandemic as tedium inhibited their sexual interest.

When treating couples with desire issues, it's important to ensure that both partners actually want to be sexual together or at all. Sometimes one or both feel obliged to be sexual or worry about being different when they're really content with their sexual behaviour.

DISCREPANCY OF DESIRE

Many couples complain of differences in their sexual interest which create problems for the relationship or distress for them as individuals. Though no longer a DSM dysfunction, it's a common reason for couples to seek sex therapy. Work on how to negotiate and communicate can often promote sexual behaviour, as can some myth busting. Men *are* often more interested in sex than women, but whether this is a biological effect or an expectation that they should be is debatable.

There's often a circular relationship dynamic too. For instance, one partner may regard sexual frequency as an indicator of their relationship's health while the other only wants sex when the relationship is clearly healthy. As low interest partners may seem to have all the control, the high interest partner often expresses feelings of rejection and resentment which the low interest partner finds unappealing.

Reasons for refusing sex can be as simple as exhaustion, poor timing or personal hygiene, so discussion about when and what sexual behaviours are possible can be very helpful. Clear boundaries actually allow *more* touch, as fear of the other partner's expectations can lead to refusal. Nonetheless, it's understandable that interest in sex will reduce when people are tired, stressed or when sexual overtures are repeatedly rebuffed. This can lead to a collusive pursuer:distancer dynamic where sex is avoided by both partners, particularly when intimacy or commitment issues exist. The high sex partner is able to claim they would be having lots of sex if it were available, while the low sex partner feels sexually desirable without having to be sexual. Couples like this often present when there's been a change in the dynamic, such as ceasing pursuit or the distancer starting to show sexual interest.

HYPOACTIVE SEXUAL DESIRE DISORDER (HSDD)

This is the DSM-5 definition of male loss of libido, which often develops as a result of other problems, such as erectile difficulties, that lead to sexual avoidance. Issues in the relationship, fears about hurting the partner and unrealistic personal expectations about sex may coexist. A number of medications and recreational drugs can affect male desire, as can some medical and mental health conditions and a history of sexual abuse or of suppressing sexual feelings. High levels of the hormone prolactin and low testosterone levels also affect desire, though it has been argued that testosterone is over-prescribed.

It's important to investigate what else has been happening since desire diminished or if it was ever there in the first place. Some people enjoy regular masturbation but have no desire for their partner, perhaps due to relational issues or lost attraction.

> **Simmering** involves encouraging a low desire partner to allow any sexual feelings to develop and subside whenever they occur, and to incorporate fantasy. This can be highly effective in promoting desire, especially if accompanied by curiosity about thoughts and feelings which accompany arousal. The individual may then be encouraged to deliberately seek arousal by remembering pleasurable sexual experiences.

Working with the relationship and both the couple's beliefs and attitudes, mindfulness, body scanning, sensate and self-focus experiments, and directing the affected partner's attention towards any glimmer of sexual feelings, can all be helpful if the couple wants to resume sex. A sex ban and/or consent experiments which produce highly boundaried sexual behaviours can provide reassurance and build confidence through graduated exposure.

SEXUAL INTEREST/AROUSAL DISORDER

This is the DSM's female version of low libido, and is most often treated successfully with psychological interventions which explore beliefs and offer personal information, combined with self and sensate focus experiments. It often develops in relation to physical events such as pregnancy, childbirth, menopause, exhaustion or a change in body image. Testosterone patches may be prescribed following **surgical menopause**, but other attempts to find pharmacological solutions have all so far failed.

Self-discovery and masturbation may be especially important in women with little sexual experience to explore what they find arousing. Sexual pain and/or inexperienced partners, whose techniques are insufficiently arousing, may have deterred some women from sex, as they may experience guilt about sexual feelings or fears about attraction and sexual response.

ERECTILE DIFFICULTIES (ED)

Almost every man experiences erectile difficulties at some time. There may be a problem getting an erection in the first place or it may not last long. This is often situational, in that it mainly or only occurs during sex with a partner, erections during solo sex often remaining unaffected. Tiredness, drugs or alcohol can affect erections, as can anxiety. A new relationship and partner conflict are especially likely to create performance anxiety. Equally, erections can disappear when relationships become closer and there is more at stake.

> *Performance anxiety* refers to fears about being able to 'perform' adequately in sexual situations. Examples include being able to get and maintain an erection, to delay ejaculation until desired, to climax or to arouse a partner.

ED is also a condition of perception. For instance, very few men under 35 complain of ED while about half of men aged over 65 do. Some expect their erections to be the same at 80 as they were at 18, though it's normal for them to be less hard as men age. Indeed, men can also be highly aroused, and even ejaculate, without an erection, and the penis need not be that hard for vaginal penetration. A longer **refractory period** after ejaculation, when another erection or orgasm isn't possible, is also normal as men age. However, even a single incident of ED can cause so much anxiety that the problem becomes chronic. It's therefore important that a thorough medical and psychosocial history is taken, as so many interacting medical, relational, social and psychological factors can contribute to ED.

Because erections occur when the arteries supplying blood to the penis dilate, and the resulting pressure on surrounding tissues and veins causes the blood to be trapped, any medical condition affecting the cardiovascular system can compromise them. Trauma from radiotherapy, surgery or spinal cord injury, for instance, can be a cause. Neurological conditions like multiple sclerosis, and endocrine conditions like diabetes, which can affect both the cardiovascular system and cause **neuropathy**, are also highly implicated. Lifestyle changes, such as giving up smoking, drinking less alcohol, improving diet, losing weight and exercising more can all be helpful, especially as these all lower blood pressure. Even if erection is satisfactorily restored, many men remain anxious. Considerable help may be needed to direct attention away from the erection and towards sensual touch and non-penetrative pleasure. The intention isn't to replace intercourse but to expand the sexual repertoire and challenge unhelpful thinking about what men should be capable of.

Medical treatments for ED itself include **PDE 5 inhibitors** like Viagra (sildenafil), Cialis (tadalafil), Levitra (vardenafil) and Spedra (avanafil) which are taken orally, can act within 20–60 minutes and remain active for several hours. They are sometimes suggested by sex therapists towards the end of therapy or when resuming intercourse, simply to restore confidence even if the erection is becoming reliable. Some people find they cause unpleasant side effects, such as a stuffy nose, indigestion, flushing and headache. Experimenting with different doses and drugs and taking folic acid usually address this, though some men reject drugs as they feel they should be able to have an erection without chemical assistance.

Other medical treatments include use of a vacuum device to create an erection, vasodilators administered in the form of creams or directly into the penis via injection or a pessary, shockwave therapy to improve blood flow and penile implants, which provide a semi-erection which is sufficient for vaginal intercourse.

WAX AND WANE

This is a confidence building exercise whereby the penis is stimulated to erection and allowed to subside two or three times before ejaculating if this is desired. Because Wax and Wane seems outcome focused – seeking erectile control – the therapist can reduce stress by asking for feedback about the client's anxiety management rather than concentrating on their erection. Mirroring their sense of achievement is important, but it's helpful to link the way the client approached the experiment and managed negative thoughts to their positive results. It's also important to approach the experiment gradually and incrementally, eventually adding different kinds of touch and maybe using an oiled hand.

When sufficient confidence is gained, the partner's touch can be introduced, noting whether this affects anxiety and how that's managed between the couple. They should be warned to expect erectile loss as they approach new experiments, though in practice ED may not occur or it may be clear why it did. Once confident with Wax and Wane, it can be practised during penetration by ceasing movement, allowing the erection to subside and letting the penis remain in the vagina/anus until the erection returns.

PAIN AND SENSATION DISORDERS

Both men and women can experience pain associated with sex for a wide variety of physical and psychological reasons, which may all ultimately result in sexual avoidance and loss of desire. Many people have spent years seeking a diagnosis and try sex therapy as a last resort. While sex therapy can undoubtedly help, it may not be appropriate to give up on medical intervention, as it can simply be a matter of finding a clinician who understands the condition. Pain caused by **endometriosis**, for example, is notoriously difficult to diagnose and treat. Similarly, many men aged over 50 experience chronic or intermittent pelvic pain for which no cause can be found. In women, chronic pelvic pain may be due to an infection such as chlamydia, so referral to a sexual health clinic is always advisable.

It can be difficult to identify the source of pain, so it may be necessary to consult different specialists, such as a urologist for bladder and prostate problems, a gynaecologist for female genital and reproductive pain, a general surgeon for bowel and gastrointestinal conditions and even neurologists and endocrinologists, especially where there is peripheral neuropathy or a suspicion of hormone issues. If there is any bloating in women with pain, or if there's back pain, changes in bowel habits, frequent urination, tummy ache or feeling full, they should be urged to visit their GP as soon as possible as these can be a sign of ovarian cancer. Complaints of pain in the middle of the menstrual cycle may be due to *mittelschmerz*, which causes one-sided abdominal pain at **ovulation**. This can last from a few hours to a few days and be accompanied by bleeding. It can be treated with drugs which prevent ovulation, though it may come and go or disappear altogether.

GENITO-PELVIC PAIN/PENETRATION DISORDER

Painful intercourse (*dyspareunia*) and **vaginismus** (difficulties with penetration) have been combined in this DSM disorder which also covers *vulvodynia*, a highly painful burning sensation in the vulva, close to the vaginal entrance which in some cases only occurs when touched (provoked vulvodynia). Referral to a skin specialist may be more appropriate than a gynaecologist for vulvodynia.

Dyspareunia often progresses to vaginismus, so it's essential to establish the nature of the pain, and how possible intercourse has become, so that appropriate medical referral can be made. While it's unethical to encourage women to attempt painful intercourse for their partner's sake, many women wish to experience penetrative sex, become pregnant or simply use tampons. Mindfulness, breathing exercises, yoga and relaxation are helpful for all pain, and daily vulval massage can help relax vaginal muscles. Some women avoid touching the vulva but, for vaginismus, self-focus exercises are necessary to promote confidence and familiarity with their anatomy. Squatting or sitting comfortably with knees bent, and using a hand mirror to watch, they can touch the vaginal entrance as they contract and relax the pelvic floor muscles, identifying how to relax them. Rhythmic breathing can also help relax abdominal and pelvic muscles and is useful for Reverse Kegel Exercises in which the person lies down comfortably, pushing the lower back downwards against the bed/floor without moving the spine or pelvis. This can be repeated five or six times as they imagine the muscles of the pelvic floor stretching with each breath. They can gradually build up the number of pushes and graduate to doing the exercise leaning against the wall or seated.

Once comfortable with Reverse Kegels and genital exploration, inserting a lubricated finger into the vagina may be attempted. Starting with the little finger and graduating to bigger fingers or more than one, it's important to be relaxed and to notice thoughts and feelings which help or interfere with the experiment. Some women may prefer to guide their partner's finger(s) or use vaginal trainers.

Vaginal trainers are plastic or silicone tubes in different sizes which can be inserted into the vagina with plenty of lubrication to accustom the individual to the sensation of penetration and reassure them. Also known as dilators, they don't actually stretch the vagina.

Starting with the smallest trainer, individuals are taught to relax and discover that penetration is possible. However, there is some evidence that use of trainers may increase anxiety, as the outcome focus may be counterproductive. Trainers can be prescribed or purchased privately in a variety of materials and colours. Vibrating trainers are also available.

Before attempting penis-in-vagina (**PiV**) sex, the couple should get used to using the penis to touch the vagina, including using it to stimulate the clitoris. Once this is well tolerated, provided there is arousal and sufficient lubrication, the woman can initially just insert the tip of the penis sitting astride her partner. If this goes well, further introduction of the penis could be attempted. The partner should be advised to stay still to allow time for relaxation of the vagina and not to thrust until instructed by the woman. To begin with, only she should control movement which should be shallow and allow simultaneous clitoral stimulation if possible, stopping if there is pain. Once intercourse is established successfully, the couple can experiment with the most comfortable positions and the partner can be more active. Couples using **strap-ons** should be especially gentle.

The partner's attitude is obviously important, as impatience or lack of understanding can compromise the whole sex therapy process. Fortunately, most couples with vaginismus seem to have established positive sexual behaviours without intercourse and are both orgasmic. They're consequently much more able to appreciate that PiV sex is not essential to pleasure and to approach experiments with cooperation and tolerance. An exception is when vaginismus has developed recently, as a result of surgery or birth trauma, for instance, or when the relationship has deteriorated. Sex therapy may be contraindicated if the relationship is insufficiently robust or the partner is intolerant of the woman's condition. Physiotherapy can replace insertion tolerance in women who are phobic or also experiencing incontinence.

Many people with pelvic pain have a history of sexual trauma or genital surgery and may respond well to treatments such as hypnotherapy or **EMDR** before attempting sex therapy.

PERSISTENT GENITAL AROUSAL DISORDER (PGAD)

Though it's more common in women, PGAD can affect men too. It involves involuntary feelings akin to sexual arousal in the genital area which are unrelieved by orgasm and are sometimes accompanied by pounding or throbbing pain. It can occur spontaneously or be triggered by touch, orgasm or clothes. A feature is that there is no subjective feeling of arousal, just sensations which occur unbidden. Sometimes there are multiple orgasms, lasting for hours or even days, which interfere with daily life and prevent sleep.

PGAD is considered to be a rare condition, which many clinicians have never heard of, and does not appear in either DSM-5 or ICD-10. However, it may be more common than is appreciated, as sufferers can be embarrassed to seek help or don't receive support when they do. Sex therapists, however, can reassure clients that PGAD will pass eventually. For instance, it sometimes occurs around the menopause and then disappears. Mindfulness, relaxation and distraction techniques may help during a PGAD episode, but more important work may be needed to reassure clients they're not abnormal and to alleviate what can be severe shame.

Sex therapists can research locally to find helpful clinicians. The epilepsy drug Pregabalin may be offered, as it treats both anxiety and neuropathic pain. Nerve blocks have also been used, as well as antidepressants and tranquillisers.

ANAL SEX

It's certainly not a dysfunction, and isn't necessarily painful, but some people seek advice about anal sex. It's not something to try on a whim and should be avoided if there are haemorrhoids, warts or sores around the anus. The receptive partner needs to be relaxed or the external anal sphincter will tighten when penetration is attempted. Preparation helps with relaxation, such as massaging the perineum prior to inserting anything. Penetration with fingers, using a finger cot, or tongue, making use of a dental dam, should be tried several times before penile intercourse is attempted. Wearing a butt plug for a few hours beforehand can also help the rectum to relax.

It's important to pause once the penis is inserted to allow time for accommodation and only gradually continue with insertion and movement. The internal anal sphincter is not under voluntary control, so time is needed for it to open. Plenty of water-based lubrication should be used, reapplying often, as lube not only assists insertion but will prevent condoms – which should always be worn for anal intercourse – from tearing or coming off.

Couples should be warned not to switch from anal to vaginal intercourse without washing the penis and applying a fresh condom if these are used for vaginal penetration. Hands and sex toys should also be washed, as there is significant risk of infection.

PEGGING

Strictly speaking, pegging refers to anal penetration of a man by a woman, but a **strap-on dildo** can be used for penetration for anyone without a penis. The same preparation is required, but even more care needs to be taken as it isn't so easy to recognise resistance, and the dildo is more rigid than a penis. Pausing for longer at the point of insertion may be necessary, as this can be uncomfortable or make the receiver fear they're about to poo. This sensation diminishes as the rectum adapts.

Small, and subsequently painful, tears can be caused by too vigorous thrusting during anal sex, which is a reason to avoid it if recreational drugs have been taken which may mask pain. Stimulation of the penis during penetration may be enjoyed, though anal play or stimulation of the prostate in men can also produce high arousal. Women's orgasm can be achieved by using a vibrating dildo or the dildo may be positioned to stimulate the clitoris.

ORGASM

The disorders of orgasm covered in the DSM are premature (early) ejaculation, delayed ejaculation and female orgasmic disorder (anorgasmia). Some conditions which cause nerve damage and some drugs impair orgasm, but the issues preventing it are often psychological. For instance, orgasm and ejaculation are not the same thing, though they usually happen at the same time. Consequently, people who can't ejaculate following, say, prostate surgery *can* still orgasm. Many of the issues people present with are about the quality of their orgasm or their ability to control when it happens.

PREMATURE (EARLY) EJACULATION (EE)

Less than a third of those who present for treatment meet the DSM criteria for early ejaculation of requiring little or no stimulation to ejaculate and ejaculating within a minute of penetration three-quarters of the time. Many people expect much longer than the estimated average of two to five minutes' thrusting, with a 'normal' time considered one to ten minutes for **PiV** sex. Ejaculation when masturbating may be much quicker. However, worried couples often aren't convinced by statistics nor the reassurance that the time taken to ejaculate not only varies from one person to another but also from one occasion to another, depending on circumstances and mood. Because those who don't meet the DSM criteria for EE can be so distressed by the belief that they do, they can still benefit from sex therapy to demonstrate there's so much more to good sex than penetration and thrusting.

There's a widespread belief that EE is a condition of inexperienced lovers and that it'll improve once the novelty of partnered sex has worn off. However, some people are just very sensitive, and EE can be lifelong. It can also be difficult to undo a habit of over-stimulating to climax quickly, which sometimes develops in boys who share a bedroom and are scared of being discovered masturbating. Worry about maintaining an erection, belief that a partner isn't as interested in sex as they are or guilt about sex are other common causes of hurrying.

Relationship difficulties often develop, especially when a partner is critical or the affected partner is desperate to make them climax, which can lead to response pressure and faking orgasm. Avoidance is common, and one or both partners may have developed low desire. Work with the couple's anxiety and beliefs about sex, combined with sensate focus, often improves their sexual experience considerably. Concentration on erection and orgasm can prevent couples from experimenting, and they may even be unaware of the affected partner's **refractory period**. Some men with EE always climax quickly, going on to have a second more satisfying orgasm later in the love-making session.

> A partner's desire to please the other, especially to 'make' them orgasm, can create response pressure in the other. It's a form of performance anxiety which can lead to someone faking orgasm as the pressure to please their partner by climaxing can make it impossible.

Clients may have tried many remedies to treat their EE, including squeezing the penis to prevent ejaculation, though this can lead to habitual seepage of ejaculate rather than more usual spurting. Local anaesthetic creams and sprays need to be washed off before unprotected intercourse or oral sex and may cause local irritation.

Medical checks should always be sought to rule out organic causes of EE, such as high testosterone levels and other endocrine conditions. PDE 5 inhibitors may be offered to see if they reduce the **refractory period** and SSRI antidepressants are often rapidly effective in prolonging the **latency period**.

STOP:START EXPERIMENT

It may be counterproductive to offer this control experiment to a very anxious and outcome-focused client, at least initially. A first, and relatively unthreatening step, is for the client to recognise their **point of inevitability**, after which ejaculation is unstoppable. Many men with EE have never recognised this moment, especially if they've habitually rushed masturbation. When the exercise is only to recognise the point of inevitability, it doesn't matter if they ejaculate, so this experiment should be repeated several times until the client volunteers experiencing comfort with doing it. Introducing the more challenging part of the experiment after this causes less anxiety and more confidence, especially as some clients will have already started experimenting with the next stage by themselves.

In the Stop:Start phase, the client is asked to masturbate almost to the point of inevitability and then stop, waiting for a moment or two before repeating the exercise. If they're also experiencing ED they should wait until the erection completely subsides before proceeding. They can then repeat this process three or four times before allowing themselves to ejaculate. As always, it's important that they report how they managed any anxiety and the presence of any negative thoughts during Stop:Start. Clients may be very disappointed if they're unable to prevent ejaculation, so it's essential to emphasise the experimental nature of the process. Advising them to change their masturbatory technique from the start, and especially to slow it down, can make a big difference. Eventually, some are simply able to slow down even more before the point of inevitability rather than stopping altogether.

Once they are thoroughly confident with this process, they can begin to experiment with their partner. The partner's touch obviously introduces another change in sensation, which can be challenging. A signal to stop stimulation when arousal is high, rather than too close to the point of inevitability, will build confidence for both. They can gradually introduce different kinds of touch, oral stimulation and genital to genital contact. It's important to be used to the sensation of the penis touching the vulva, especially as this may previously have led to ejaculation. Indeed, EE may still return when insertion is anticipated, and couples should be warned that this is possible.

If they do wish to experiment with intercourse, they should avoid thrusting and allow the penis to 'rest' in the vagina/anus for a moment after insertion. As confidence grows, the couple can experiment further with a variety of sexual positions and also possibly have short bursts of intercourse interspersed with other forms of lovemaking. By this time, they should have learned more about what they both enjoy and what causes their orgasms, whilst being much less outcome-focused. The affected partner may find that their orgasms become more intense as a result of the Stop:Start process **edging** them towards climax.

INDIVIDUAL THERAPY FOR EE

Clients who consider they have EE often present without their partner, due to embarrassment and belief that the issue is entirely their concern. However, though individual therapy can help them to recognise the point of inevitability and improve confidence in their control, it's not possible to predict how this will transfer to partnered sex or to know how supportive partners are without meeting them. It's therefore important to be positive but realistic about what's possible. Some clients have only ever had casual relationships due to concern about their EE, so therapy may need to continue for some time if they wish to start a longer relationship.

DELAYED EJACULATION (DE)

The DSM classifies DE as inability or difficulty in reaching ejaculation or orgasm at least three-quarters of the time, despite adequate stimulation. Neurological conditions and prescribed medication/recreational drugs are among the most common causes of DE, so medical checks are advisable, particularly if DE occurs when masturbating. However, there are often complex psychological reasons why ejaculation isn't occurring, often related to guilt about sex, welfare of the partner or fear of pregnancy. Sometimes, the person just isn't aroused, which may be due to relationship difficulties or frequent porn use having made partnered sex less exciting. A common issue is an idiosyncratic masturbatory style which is difficult to reproduce in partnered sex. Sex therapy can therefore be highly successful in facilitating experiments in arousal and technique.

It's especially important to proceed slowly and mindfully so that the client doesn't just reproduce old habits, imposing a complete sex ban which includes masturbation and avoidance of pornography until the arousal phase of treatment. The client also needs to be able to concentrate on their own interests rather than being excessively concerned about their partner's pleasure. Sensual touching without attempting to arouse increases sensuality and intimacy while reducing focus on outcome. Later in the process, satisfactory sexual experiences with or without ejaculation will reinforce this. Once the couple realise that ejaculation isn't always necessary for a good sexual experience, it may become more likely. Many sex therapists suggest orgasmic triggers, such as tensing and relaxing, if orgasm seems close. However, this focus on outcome can sometimes become counterproductive.

It's not unusual for a client to have been unconcerned about DE until recently, particularly if they or their partners framed it as having good control or didn't realise it was unusual. Sex therapy may be sought when a couple want a pregnancy or when a new partner is finding sex painful. Some couples describe bruising and exhaustion, and a pattern of the affected partner eventually masturbating after half an hour or more of intercourse.

FEMALE ORGASMIC DISORDER

Many women don't climax every time they have partnered sex, yet still enjoy their experience and aren't distressed by this. They often present for therapy in a new relationship where it's really the partner who is concerned and the woman wants to please them. The DSM sees the problem as existing when orgasm fails three-quarters of the time for more than six months. It can be helpful to explore what's different on any occasions orgasm occurs. Sometimes, it's the context that makes all the difference, such as being on holiday, less stressed or when the relationship is going well. Many clients have never made this link.

Only about 10 per cent of women have never climaxed at all. Some are climaxing but don't recognise what's happening as orgasm. This can be because they've applied a fierce vibrator directly to the clitoris, and the intensity of their orgasm has not been particularly pleasant. Others have been led to believe that 'real' orgasms happen with a partner or during intercourse and are worried when their orgasms are no better or non-existent. A sign that orgasm has occurred would be that touching the clitoris directly afterwards can be uncomfortable.

Even now, with improved access to sexual information, some people believe good sex requires spontaneous intercourse involving 'earth-shattering' simultaneous orgasm. *Any* orgasm is rare for most women during **PiV** sex, with a mere 15–20 per cent thought to regularly orgasm during intercourse, while the vast majority require additional clitoral stimulation to climax. Some people worry that they take too long to climax, which is often due to being tired, distracted, too much alcohol or anxiety. Others are concerned that the quality of their orgasm seems changed. Causes include endocrine and neurological conditions, anxiety, menopause and hysterectomy, as womb contractions during orgasm can contribute to pleasure. Some women experience gripey pain with or following orgasm after the menopause.

It's important to establish the client's comfort with their bodies and previous sexual experience, including frequency of orgasm with masturbation. Sometimes a partner's poor technique can close down sexual expectation and desire, as can sexual or relational abuse. The impact of any traumatic events may be relevant, and treatments such as **EMDR** may be necessary before sex therapy.

Cognitive restructuring and psychoeducation are important from the beginning, with the therapist modelling and encouraging curiosity and discouraging binary thinking. Self-focus exercises should be begun early, building up to a masturbatory programme experimenting with self-touch, erotica and sex toys while continuing sensual touching experiments with the partner. The partner's positive and understanding attitude is crucial. Partners who feel blamed, are blaming or resentful make a relaxed experience unlikely.

Women and their partners should be advised to take arousal slowly and leave the clitoris alone until arousal starts to build. Exploration of erogenous zones during sensate focus can be augmented by the woman's own self-discovery. Many avoid their nipples and vulva, which can be a source of considerable pleasure, for instance. Self-touch during partnered sex should be encouraged, particularly when *being* touched creates self-consciousness.

Pretending to climax, holding the breath and letting it go and performing Kegel exercises (see Chapter 3) are among orgasmic triggers. Using a vibrator to become aroused and then continuing with fingers can be helpful to some women. Generally, though, a temporary orgasm ban with partnered sex, and an instruction to notice their arousal, can remove pressure and lead to 'surprise' orgasms. Those who experience considerable guilt about enjoying sex may benefit from role play, which may allow them to experience pleasure in the role. However, the quality of their relationship, feelings about themselves and their beliefs about sex may turn out to be the most significant factors in treating anorgasmia.

HUMAN SEXUAL RESPONSE

The sex researchers William Masters and Virginia Johnson proposed a largely linear model for sexual response which was based on laboratory studies of people having sex. Working mainly in the 1960s and 1970s they proposed that sexual arousal was followed by a brief plateau phase when bodily changes stabilised, followed by the peak of arousal – orgasm – and then resolution, as the body returned to its usual state. Because this was accepted, any deviations from this model could be seen as problematic. Yet the descriptions of 'problems' above demonstrate that sexual response is not actually linear. Some of the problems we treat are only problematic because we think they are or because we believe that finding solutions indicates there's a problem. For instance, we know that erections are more likely to come and go during lovemaking as we age, but this doesn't necessarily mean we aren't aroused or interested.

While the **Masters and Johnson** model was in many ways liberating, as it confirmed what was 'normal', this created the pressure to be very normal – to become aroused on cue and to proceed through the stages without variation. At the time, there was some hostility to the idea that women didn't need men to climax, so Masters and Johnson allowed the myth that intercourse could produce orgasm in any woman. This is theoretically true but also not reliably true, as most women don't. Another takeaway has been that men are finished following orgasm, as their resolution phase returns their penis to a flaccid state, while women have capacity to go on to further orgasms if stimulation continues. Consequently, many straight couples' lovemaking involves trying to make the woman climax, preferably more than once, so that the man can get on with his orgasm. This creates response pressure in women, who may not be able to climax simply because they know it's required.

As if this wasn't enough, sex psychologist Helen Singer Kaplan added desire ahead of arousal in the cycle. Problems with desire, she thought, were due to deep-seated emotional and psychological issues, providing us with one more area to have problems with. We now know that desire does not always precede arousal and, in fact, *only* follows arousal in some people. We also now know that it's difficult to experience desire when we're tired, worried, hungry, busy or distracted. So while the human sexual response cycle reflected some great research, it's unfortunate that it has influenced most people's beliefs about what's okay. As sex therapists, we can offer a more nuanced and realistic view. As you'll see from the topics below, there are many more issues than physiological response feeding into people's ability to be sexual, often related to beliefs and anxiety. Indeed, Masters and Johnson ultimately recognised this and created the first sex therapy programmes, based on CBT.

BODY ISSUES

DSM-5 classes *Body Dysmorphic Disorder* as an obsessive compulsive condition whereby someone spends inordinate amounts of time worrying about a minor or non-existent flaw. Though most people's body concerns don't amount to an obsession, they can be extremely inhibiting and cause considerable distress.

Any change in our bodies can affect the way we feel about ourselves, either boosting confidence or creating negative beliefs and self-consciousness. Few people who acquire a negative body image present for therapy with this as their sexual problem, yet this alone may be causing them to avoid sex or distracting them from their pleasure when they do. Many couples who believe their partners have lost interest are unaware that they've actually just lost confidence. Consequently, how people feel about their bodies should always be investigated more than once in assessment, as many are reluctant to admit how much their negative body image is affecting them.

INEXPERIENCE

Sometimes very inexperienced couples present with unrealistic ideas about sex and what they believe should be possible. They've often been removed from school sex education classes and genuinely have very little knowledge. Sometimes their unhelpful ideas are so deeply ingrained that they don't believe sex therapists when they try to normalise their experience. For instance, they may have romantic notions that being in love should make sex work well. They may have no idea about what arouses them or only respond to touch developed in solo sex. Often, they're too embarrassed to show their partner what they like.

However, it's not just sexually inexperienced couples who aren't familiar with their own bodies. A 2021 study into public understanding of genital anatomy found that most people, including women, were unable to identify female genital anatomy. There was particular confusion between the clitoris and urethra. This may be because biology textbooks concentrate on reproductive rather than genital anatomy. Indeed, most people confuse the vulva with the vagina.

Inexperienced couples often don't know that arousal and lubrication are needed before penetration or expect that thrusting can continue indefinitely until they simultaneously orgasm. What they do know may have been gleaned from chats with equally poorly informed friends or from pornography. This can sometimes give them misguided ideas about what is liked or acceptable during sex, including a view that violence should be included. Obviously, not all porn viewed creates this impression but it's a safeguarding issue we can't ignore, especially with younger clients. They may also both be surprised that their bodies are unlike those of the porn actors, and feel inadequate as a result. Men may have concerns about the volume and strength of ejaculate, as well as penis size and shape. Breasts and labia may be of concern to women. With their consent, it can be helpful to show them pictures of a variety of breasts and genitals, demonstrating that normal is quite a spectrum.

Some inexperienced couples are under pressure from their families to have a baby, which may add to their feelings of difference. Therapists whose manner is containing and normalising of *their* experience, however wide of the mark that may be, are usually rewarded by their clients' diligence and positivity. Nonetheless, the work may initially seem slow as they overcome any disappointment and tune into new ways of thinking and behaving.

PREGNANCY AND CHILDBIRTH

Many couples seek sex therapy in order to have a baby, so can be advised to return for further help once they're pregnant or afterwards if they have any remaining issues. Sex therapists sometimes won't work with pregnant clients because their bodies are going through such profound changes, and advise them to return a year after the birth. But during and post-pregnancy is precisely when many couples need support. Sometimes it's just a matter of normalising their experience and offering some psychoeducation about what to expect. It's also a way of picking up on depression in either parent which can begin antenatally or up to a year after the birth, peaking at three to six months. Fathers are more likely to be affected if their partners have postnatal depression too, but it can just affect them.

Some people are put off by their partner's shape during pregnancy or by beliefs that it's inappropriate for mothers to be sexual. While some women feel more sexy during pregnancy, and their bodies become more responsive, others are affected by nausea, exhaustion and other pregnancy symptoms, and don't feel sexual at all. Weight gain, loose ligaments and postural changes can make usual exercise difficult or dangerous. When someone uses exercise to assist mood regulation, this can be really challenging. Indeed, all changes to routine, including stopping work, could affect well-being, as we often don't realise how small habits or routines help until they're gone.

After the birth, both partners are often anxious about resuming sexual contact. Breasts may look very different, with a train track of veins, and leak milk during sex. There's obviously weight to lose and abdominal muscles can feel uncomfortable. Internal stitches can be infuriatingly irritating. *Any* tears or stitches need to heal, and bleeding should have ceased, before intercourse can be attempted. New mums are usually advised to wait at least six weeks, but that may seem quite soon for some exhausted parents. Bruising can remain for up to three months, and the vagina and vulva may look and feel very different for some time. Pelvic floor exercises (Kegels) should be started as soon as possible as this helps prevent incontinence and restore vaginal tone, though some change is likely to be permanent. Women should seek medical advice if discomfort persists, rather than assuming it's just due to anxiety or needs more time to settle. Sometimes women's tears haven't healed correctly, have been poorly stitched or they may need physiotherapy or pelvic repair. Even if all's well, reassurance can make a huge difference.

Oestrogen levels fall dramatically after the birth and adjusting can account for so-called baby blues which often arrive as milk production replaces colostrum around three days after the birth. Breastfeeding reduces libido and can make the vagina dry and sore, so water-based lubrication may be needed to assist penetration.

This is quite a lot to deal with but, rather than just putting off any form of intimacy, couples can be advised to create boundaries to agree what *is* possible. Reviewing this regularly means that even if the occasional hug is as much as can be managed initially, physical touch can gradually be built up in a planned and consensual way. Just giving sex a go when a couple are tipsy often doesn't go well and they're then put off.

Without some consideration and planning it's easy for sex to seem too much like hard work, so many couples present some years after their families are complete, having made love very little since their first pregnancy. The relationship may also have been deteriorating since then. Couples may have found it difficult to adjust to the focus on the baby, and either partner may feel left out. Thereafter, children are around all the time, making it hard for couples to find time and space for their relationship.

FERTILITY

Sex is a frequent casualty of fertility treatment, as it becomes associated with monthly failure and disappointment. Even successful couples can become focused on outcome – pregnancy – and then be blindsided by the realities of a baby at a time when they need space to recover from the ordeal of treatment and, sometimes, repeated losses. Many couples' hopes are dashed when pregnancies don't go to term and find it hard to resume sex knowing it previously led to a miscarriage or neonatal death. Some approach sex therapy still coming to terms with the reality that they won't be able to have their own child, while others with children want to repair sexual issues which developed as a result of their fertility journey.

Couples often feel raw and vulnerable, and need sensitive support to move forward in their own time. It's even harder if one is resentful about quitting treatment, feeling misunderstood or different as a result of needing assisted conception. Some therapists feel a need to fix such couples and try to conduct the work too quickly, often missing important factors in the relationship. For instance, some men, in particular, are unable to show their grief as they feel the need to 'be strong' for their partner. Some partners will even end the relationship rather than show the distress of baby loss, feeling relationship breakup is somehow more acceptable.

AGEING

Some couples expect sexual interest to wane as they age, and are comfortable without sex in their relationship. Others experience a renewal of interest and are prompted to seek support due to life events like retirement, an inheritance, the loss of parents or their own ill-health. Some older clients have divorced or been widows and are in new relationships, sometimes exploring a different sexual identity. They may be dating or sexually active for the first time in years and need advice about safer sex as well as help with perceived problems. Such clients present alone and may be reluctant to involve partners, though most are willing to participate. Some are reclaiming their sexuality after difficult or abusive relationships and may be surprised by how emotional this transition can be.

Prioritising their relationship as children become more independent or leave home can bring some couples into therapy. As their own family roles change, the relationship may also be adjusting to work stresses and care of elderly parents. For some couples, sex may have become dull and repetitive. Relationship psychologist David Schnarch said many couples only have *deficit sex*, which is the moves that remain once they've excluded whatever they feel their partner dislikes. What's irritating or not of interest during one sexual encounter may be super-sexy in another, but embarrassment often prevents couples from discussing their preferences or fears about each other's interests. Creating space for sex and openness about personal desires can reboot sex for couples whose intimacy has drifted away.

Unfortunately, other challenges like menopause may be exacerbating their issues. Menopause itself refers to the end of periods, which generally happens around age 51, but perimenopausal symptoms can begin much earlier and continue after periods cease. Symptoms which challenge sexual expression include hot flushes, night sweats, heavy periods, vaginal dryness, weight gain and brain fog, all of which can feel distinctly unsexy and make snuggling up particularly undesirable. Ovulation is when many women experience desire, so they may assume their libido has gone forever when they no longer feel this sexual interest. Moreover, couples with a relationship lasting more than ten years are more likely to have *responsive* rather than spontaneous desire, which requires some sort of cognitive, physical or visual stimulation. This may be more obvious in menopausal women whose symptoms affect feelings of attractiveness, but can also affect men.

GPs may offer hormone replacement therapy, vaginal lube and antidepressants to manage symptoms. Therapists can help couples rediscover their sexual triggers and deliberately make time for sex and intimacy. The exercise below may be useful for therapists as well as their clients to think about how self-image and behaviours can change unnoticed. Work on communication can make a big difference to the relationship overall, as well as to sex.

SEX THEN AND NOW

The questions in this section relate to how you felt at the beginning of your relationship.

- What made you feel attractive?
- What sexual behaviours made you feel most alive?
- How did you initiate sex?
- What made you feel close?
- What sexual behaviours did you most enjoy?

The questions in this section relate to how you feel now.

- Has how you identify sexually changed (e.g., used to identify as straight, now as bisexual)?
- How do you initiate sex?
- What makes you feel distant from your partner?
- Is there anything about sex that you miss?
- What would make the biggest difference to your sexual relationship?

G SPOT

The G spot is supposedly a small spongey area found about two to three inches inside the upper vaginal wall. Stimulating it with fingers (in a beckoning or windscreen wiper motion), sex toys or a penis may cause intense pleasure. It doesn't seem to be present or accessible in all vaginas, however, and is actually part of the clitoris. The external clitoris is only a tiny part of the much larger clitoral complex which extends internally either side of the external clitoris, rather like a wishbone. It's an extremely intricate sensory network which is unlikely to be the same in any two women. This makes it doubtful that the G spot, if it exists, could be reliably accessed in all women, as it may be elsewhere or buried too deeply within the body to be stimulated. Those with a more superficial clitoral network may be easier to stimulate, and they may be the ones more likely to orgasm as a result of penetration alone. They may also be more likely to 'squirt', as the number of women capable of squirting appears to be about 10 per cent, not dissimilar to the number able to orgasm reliably and regularly with penetration alone.

Squirting may be achieved by G spot stimulation or direct stimulation of the Skene's glands situated around the urethra (U spot). Some people think they *are* the G spot. There's also an A spot a couple of inches above the G spot, behind the cervix, which some people say is the real G spot. Each spot has been claimed to be the female equivalent of the prostate. It's also been claimed and disproved, and claimed again, that squirting is the same as female ejaculation and that the composition of squirted matter is the same as female ejaculate – clear, straw coloured or white, depending on who did the research.

We can take from this that women's bodies have great capacity for pleasure and that experimentation is indicated. Unfortunately, claims that all women can squirt or find their G spot if they try hard enough are unlikely to be correct, and just add another layer of performance pressure.

HYGIENE

Some partners are undoubtedly put off by the other's cleanliness or habits, but most hygiene issues are personal. A partner feels sweaty, has morning breath or is just longing for a shower when the other starts hugging and kissing them, so embarrassment makes them push away. The partner looking for a hug probably has no idea why this happened and just feels rejected. The 'grubby' one doesn't explain. In the end, the couple are barely touching at all ....

When little sex is happening it's always worth asking about hygiene at an early stage in the therapy process, as this is an easily resolvable communication issue. There may be other problems too, but it's surprising how much difference this conversation can have.

ILLNESS

Disability and illness can make a huge difference to sexual self-image and interest, as partners may feel afraid of hurting or that sex is inappropriate. As always, negotiating and renegotiating what's possible promotes intimacy, preventing each partner from feeling alone with their situation. Sometimes partners are frightened of seeing or showing a scar and may need to arrange clothing to protect sensitive areas until they feel comfortable naked. This is not to be rushed, as both partners need to agree pace. Partners should try to avoid slipping into the role of carer, which makes it more difficult to switch into lover mode at bedtime.

With some research, sex therapists can offer practical advice about comfortable positions for sex, including wheelchair sex, and sex aids for those who no longer find it easy to hold vibrators or have lost sensation. Many need safer sex and hygiene information. Sex is still possible for people with spinal cord injuries, though patience and experimentation may be required. Some develop sensitivity at the site of their injury and other erogenous zones which may be caressed to orgasm.

Prostate conditions offer a particular challenge, as they can be a nuisance, with symptoms such as frequent night time weeing. However, treatment, especially for cancer, can profoundly affect sexual functioning, causing nerve damage which can result in ED, incontinence, low libido and lost sensation. Orgasm may feel different and may no longer be accompanied by ejaculation. Those who formerly enjoyed stimulation of the prostate, such as through anal sex, may experience grief. Insertive partners may find their erection becomes insufficient for anal sex, though the resumption of masturbation, partnered sex and Kegel exercises (see Chapter 3) may help to restore function or prevent further deterioration.

Where couples are referred as a result of a recent medical issue, surgery or an accident, it's important to assess the couple's adaptability and problem-solving skills to see if they have realistic expectations about what is now possible. It may not be appropriate to expect the sexual relationship to be exactly the same as it was before, nor for a partner to spontaneously be interested in practices that were previously no-go. Therapists may need to find out and explain how the condition may affect sexual functioning, emphasising the importance of discussing the effects of the illness or disability rather than avoiding it. Sexology professor Paul Enzlin says patients generally go through four stages. To begin with they can't even think about sex; then they begin to wonder whether sex might still be possible; then attempts are made to re-establish sex; and, finally sex once again becomes part of the couple's life.

PERIOD SEX

Some couples say they haven't done their touching experiments because 'it was period week'. Not only is this predictable, but menstruation doesn't need to interfere with sex therapy experiments or sex. Aside from during intercourse, a period is unlikely to get in the way, as a fresh tampon can be worn so long as nothing else is inserted in the vagina. If cramps and feeling generally run down are off-putting in the first couple of days of menstruation, couples can be encouraged to find non-sexual ways to touch and be intimate. But some people feel incredibly horny during their period and also find orgasms help alleviate cramps.

Those who want to have intercourse during a period need to remember to remove their tampon, protect the bed with an old towel and wear a condom, as sexually transmitted infections can be spread more easily via blood. It's also still possible to become pregnant, particularly towards the end of a period as sperm can stay alive for many days and be present at ovulation, even if this is a week or so later. Sex in the shower is a popular way to manage mess, but won't prevent pregnancy.

It's important to look out for coercion about period sex. Some women look forward to a week off sex when they have partners who seek sex more than they want it, and some partners see it as a reason to ask for oral sex. A belief in their entitlement to sex from one partner should trigger conversations about consent, respect and responsibility for one's own sexual experience.

BLUE BALLS

A build-up of blood in the genital area after a long period of arousal can sometimes cause a sensation of heaviness or achiness, often referred to as 'blue balls'. Ceasing arousal or climaxing relieves the sensation, but it isn't dangerous and can't cause physical damage. Blue balls are sometimes used to coerce partners into sex, persuading them that it causes extreme suffering. Sex therapists can reassure couples that it would be a medical emergency if the testicles actually turned blue, as the blood supply would be cut off, the opposite of what's happening. Masturbation is a great way to relieve discomfort.

COGNITIVE ISSUES

It's clear that issues about the body are very much cognitive issues too, and the body also reacts to the way we think. And though body image obviously affects people's sense of self, the way we think about ourselves can make quite a difference to our ability or willingness to be sexual.

THE HONEYMOON PERIOD

When asked what they want from therapy, many couples say they're aiming to recapture the heady excitement of the early days when they were enthralled with one another and couldn't get enough sex. Unfortunately, that's just not possible. When we're in a new relationship, we're also in a biochemical process which intensifies feelings. As well as increasing oestrogen, progesterone and attraction enhancing pheromones, we also have more of hormones like *oxytocin* which makes us bond, *vasopressin*, which increases intensity, and *dopamine* which gives us a hit that makes us want more. Known as 'the cuddle hormone', oxytocin is also produced when breastfeeding and makes us want to bond. Combined with vasopressin, it helps us to appreciate and see the positives in our love object and to dismiss doubts. *Serotonin* makes us feel calm and euphoric, as well as more confident, a feeling that may be attributed to the partner: 'With them, I feel I could do anything'.

This chemical concoction is nature's way of making us commit, after which hormones fade out. Indeed, couples often date the start of their relationship decline to the time they moved in together or started a pregnancy, for instance. Even so, the honeymoon rarely lasts longer than three years at the absolute outside. Though they can't regain the hormones' full effect, couples can promote *some* of it by joint activities, which boost vasopressin, and making love, which triggers oxytocin. This is why couples usually feel closer and a little elated for a couple of days after sex.

Some people believe that the honeymoon period, also known as New Relationship Energy (see also pages 14 and 121), would persist if they were *really* in love, and they present for therapy worried that there's something wrong. Those whose disappointment causes them to end the relationship often assume they've made poor relationship choices, been unlucky, that there's something wrong with *them* or that partners in general are not to be trusted, any of which may bring them into therapy.

LIMERENCE

Some people habitually end relationships when the honeymoon period wanes, but are driven to seek new relationships immediately. This may be because the euphoric feelings they experience distract them from more unpleasant mood dips. Psychologist Dorothy Tennov identified an often obsessive form known as 'limerence', a state in which someone thinks and fantasises excessively about their love object. In this state they can be quite delusional about the nature of the relationship and often seek therapy to go over and over possible signs that their feelings are reciprocated, even after it has been clearly stated that they are not.

Sexual feelings aren't always involved, but the person's state of arousal can be very high and physically manifested with sweating, rapid pulse, dry mouth, light-headedness and brain fog. When this happens in a relationship, there can be extreme fears of rejection and expectations which the other partner may find overwhelming. Because those affected fantasise so much, they can be disappointed and distressed when the partner doesn't live up to their dreams. Though they make excuses for this, ultimately they may develop chronic blaming and be so distressed that the partner fears ending the relationship. Alternatively, they may adore from afar, with the object of their adoration completely unaware. In extreme cases, admirers may develop stalking or revenge behaviour when they feel let down.

FAKING ORGASMS

Research suggests nearly half of all women have faked an orgasm, compared with only about a fifth of men. Women often do it to please their partner and/or end intercourse. Sometimes this is because they're just not in the mood for sex and sometimes it's because the partner believes they need intercourse to orgasm. Clearly, they're not actually getting the stimulation they need to do so, but some women allow this because they feel they ought to be able to orgasm this way or because it means so much to their partner that they do. This can become a problem when it regularly happens early in a relationship and develops into an established pattern. If what began as a pleasant casual encounter develops into a relationship, it can be difficult to change that pattern.

Sometimes someone pretends that orgasm problems have just begun when they want to change some aspects of lovemaking but don't want to let their partner know they've been faking. If they attend sex therapy, this will usually come out in the individual history taking, though sometimes people don't let on. Men with delayed ejaculation may fake, so DE should be investigated if they reveal this. However, it's also often just an occasional practice when someone is tired or tipsy.

When either partner discovers the other has been faking, there can be feelings of disbelief and betrayal. It helps to remind them that the motivation for faking is generally the avoidance of hurt feelings. A broader conversation may nevertheless be needed about trust, communication and why we feel we have to orgasm every time we make love anyway.

MINDFULNESS

Helping people to move out of their heads and tune into their bodies can be surprisingly difficult. Some people use considerable energy to avoid noticing unpleasant feelings in their bodies, particularly those associated with anxiety and grief, so they aren't comfortable with body scanning. On the other hand, people who believe bodily feelings indicate that something is wrong may become even more convinced of problems if they body scan. This can be overcome by linking bodily feelings with thoughts and emotions. This is a CBT intervention which allows people to notice more about their own experiencing, and can be extremely helpful during sex therapy both for appreciating sensual touch and arousal and for becoming aware of intrusive or unhelpful thoughts.

Mindfulness exercises encourage controlled breathing, body awareness and guided imagery to move attention away from unhelpful or anxious thoughts and to relax. They generally begin with breathing exercises, often involving a deep breath in and a longer breath out. This immediately calms by engaging the parasympathetic nervous system. Body awareness may be encouraged by imagining the breath flowing through different body parts, all the way from head to toe. Any intrusive thoughts are dealt with by imagining the thoughts as clouds drifting away or floating along a fast flowing river.

CULTURE

Much of what we 'believe' or consider 'normal' is a result of ideas absorbed from our surroundings. People's ethnicity, religion and community inevitably impact the way they see the world and how they should think and behave, but the way we're brought up and attitudes of our families also create 'scripts' which we refer to unconsciously. Someone may be quite certain that, say, fantasising about their favourite film star while they make love to their partner is wrong. But if the fantasy helps them orgasm, suppressing it could end up negatively affecting the lovemaking for both partners. Clients are often surprised to find they don't know where such sexual rules come from, and may even discover they resent them. Curiosity around this can be highly liberating and enable clients to make considered choices about their thoughts and behaviour rather than just assuming everyone has the same rules. A frequent feeling in clients is that they don't measure up to these arbitrary rules, especially in relation to issues like sexual frequency. Sometimes, they're clear that an idea has grown from an experience or discussion, but most often they just exist without any thought-through rationale.

People have such rules about all sorts of intersecting contexts which may affect one another in surprising ways. For instance, a couple with some money worries may find sex is affected because, say, one believes they should be the breadwinner and provide for the other. Worrying about anything could put someone off sex, but some men feel their masculinity is challenged and this may end up affecting their erections or feelings about their sexual performance. Their partner may be entirely unaware, not feel the financial problems were remotely the other's fault and see sex as a way of compensating for their problems. The two have completely different ways of looking at their issues, but may not even be aware of the way their beliefs are affecting them, let alone that their partner sees it all differently.

Clinical psychologist Alison Roper-Hall and systemic therapist John Burnham discussed what they called Social Grraaaccceeessss, an acronym for contexts that could be helpful to explore when considering the way they affect people. Contexts include: **G**ender, **G**eography, **R**ace, **R**eligion, **A**ge, **A**bility, **A**ppearance, **C**lass, **C**ulture, **C**olour, **E**thnicity, **E**ducation, **E**mployment, **S**exuality, **S**exual orientation, **S**pirituality and **S**ize. However, this is by no means an exhaustive list of the contexts which could be affecting our clients. The attitudes of families of origin can also be hugely influential, as can social media, so it's always worth checking the source of information clients have as well as the ideas they subscribe to.

Some of the scripts people follow include common myths such as The Male Sex Drive Discourse which portrays men as always being ready for sex, or even damaged if they don't have it regularly. Women, meanwhile, are positioned as needing sex for intimacy, which creates a transactional sexual relationship, whereby women trade sexual favours for closeness. It's consequently worth exploring and noting beliefs which emerge during sex therapy assessment and beyond, offering psychoeducation where appropriate and trying to connect ways each couple's relationship is affected.

CHAPTER SUMMARY

- Sex therapists need to be familiar with sexual dysfunctions described in the DSM.
- Cognitive and body related issues can impact sex by themselves or exacerbate DSM dysfunctions, sometimes in surprising ways.

FURTHER READING

Brochmann, N. & Støkken Dahl, E. (2018) *The Wonder Down Under*, London: Yellow Kite.

Campbell, C. (2018) *Love and Sex in a New Relationship*, Abingdon, UK: Routledge.

Castle, D.J. & Abel, K.M. (eds) (2016) *Comprehensive Women's Mental Health*, Cambridge, UK: Cambridge University Press.

Gurney, K. (2020) *Mind The Gap: The Truth about Desire and How to Future-proof Your Sex Life*, London: Headline Publishing.

Tennov, D. (1999) *Love and Limerence*, Lanham, MD: Scarborough House.

Wylie, K. (2015) *ABC of Sexual Health*, 3rd edn, Chichester, UK: Wiley-Blackwell.

Zilbergeld, B. (1999) *The New Male Sexuality*, New York: Bantam Books.

BIBLIOGRAPHY

American Psychiatric Association (2013) *Diagnostic and Statistical Manual of Mental Health Disorders*, 5th edn, Arlington, VA: APA.

Brewer, G. & Tidy, P. (2017) Premature ejaculation: Therapist perspectives, *Sexual & Relationship Therapy*, 32(1), 22–35.

Burnham, J. (2012) Developments in Social GRRRAAACCEEESSS: Visible–invisible and voiced–unvoiced. In Krause, I.B. (ed.), *Culture and Reflexivity in Systemic Psychotherapy: Mutual Perspectives*, London: Karnac, 139–160.

El-Hamamsy, D., Parmar, C. & Shoop-Worrall, S. *et al.* (2021) Public understanding of female genital anatomy and pelvic organ prolapse (POP): A questionnaire-based pilot study, *International Urogynecology Journal*. https://doi.org/10.1007/s00192-021-04727-9. Accessed August 30, 2021.

Enzlin, P. (2014) Sexuality in the context of chronic illness. In: Binik, Y.M. & Hall, K.S.K. (eds), *Principles and Practice of Sex Therapy*, 5th edn, New York: Guilford, 436–456.

Frith, H. (2015) *Orgasmic Bodies*, Basingstoke, UK: Palgrave Macmillan.

Hollway, W. (1984) Women's power in heterosexual sex, *Women's Studies International Forum*, 7(1), 63–68.

Lloyd, E.A. (2005) *The Case of the Female Orgasm: Bias in the Science of Evolution*, Cambridge, MA: Harvard University Press.

Macey, K., Gregory, A., Nunns, D. & das Nair, R. (2015) Women's experiences of using vaginal trainers (dilators) to treat vaginal penetration difficulties diagnosed as vaginismus: A qualitative interview study. *BMC Women's Health* 15, 49. https://bmcwomenshealth.biomedcentral.com/articles/10.1186/s12905-015-0201-6. Accessed January 23, 2022.

Wincze, J.P. & Weisberg, R.B. (2015) *Sexual Dysfunction: A Guide for Assessment and Treatment*, 3rd edn, New York: Guilford.

3

SOLUTIONS

The way fully qualified sex therapists work may depend on their setting. In private practice, therapists tend to respond to client need, gaining additional specialist training to enable them to work in more depth with, say, sexual dependency or sexual trauma. Some are trained or prefer to focus more on the state of the general relationship, and how that's affecting sex, rather than with the sexual relationship. Others work more with individuals, particularly around issues of sexuality or gender identity. Some agencies have particular ways of practising that their therapists are expected to follow, and those working in the NHS may work mainly with individuals and have fewer, and shorter, sessions.

CBT MODEL

Many of the trainings expect students to begin working with clients relatively quickly, especially if they already have considerable relationship therapy experience. This can mean beginning a process with clients before knowing how it will end. This is particularly true of those using a CBT model, where the depth of the work is in overcoming blocks to progress. The assessment process needs to be thorough to assist in anticipating blocks, and it also helps in building a therapeutic relationship and offering psychoeducation where appropriate.

In choosing CBT as the model of choice for sex therapy, Virginia Johnson recognised its use in managing anxiety, challenging or reframing unhelpful thinking and offering behavioural experiments which gave clients graduated exposure to anxiety-provoking

DOI: 10.4324/9781003265641-4

experiences. In learning to manage these and becoming used to them, anxiety diminishes. Clients, and even their therapists, sometimes mistake sex therapy experiments for exercises which just need to be worked through and ticked off. However, it's the learning from the exercises, and the opportunity they provide for psychoeducation and reframing during feedback, which makes the difference. Consequently, couples should not be hurried through the process, however impatient they are to move on.

ASSESSMENT

Similarly, assessment is an integral part of the sex therapy process which shouldn't be rushed. At no stage should it be viewed as simply a tick box exercise. The therapist's curiosity is essential to elicit information the client may not have thought relevant, and this is also an excellent opportunity for psychoeducation. Moreover, the process encourages clients to really think about their experience and what's affecting it, often seeing what's happened differently as they hear themselves speak. The therapist's interventions help clients to separate from their habitual narrative and develop their own curiosity.

INITIAL ASSESSMENT (IA)

Though couples may already have provided information over the phone or on forms, the IA occurs when the individual or couple meet their therapist for the first time. The therapist may have already begun hypothesising about the couple's situation, and this will continue during the IA when careful listening and curiosity will be used to explore further. Issues often turn out to be more complicated than the couple's presentation would originally suggest. For instance, they may say their problem is infrequent sex or low/discrepant desire; only when questioned further may they reveal insecurity about erections, unreliable orgasms or some form of pain. It's helpful to understand how each partner views their problem, when it started and what they've already tried to fix it. Often, the fixes are now contributing to the problem. If, for example, sexual initiation often results in rejection or annoyance, a partner may leave it to the other to initiate sex, resulting in no intimate touch at all in case it's thought to signal sexual interest.

Details of each partner's health and medication are useful at this stage, as they may be causing or contributing to their issues. How the couple interact and whether they feel their relationship has any other problems is also useful to know. Sometimes the issue is something as simple as having a pet in the bedroom. Many couples don't realise sex was affected when they acquired a puppy or kitten which is now sleeping with them.

This first meeting is also an opportunity to explain the sex therapy process and, if they haven't done this already, advise clients to consult their GP to check for organic causes. Some couples arrive anticipating a problem prior to body altering surgery or having a medical condition which may affect sex at some point. They may only need one session for advice and reassurance or they may want to improve their sexual relationship before any further problems develop.

HISTORY TAKING

Following the IA, couples are seen individually for a detailed history taking which should look at their personal sexual experience, their relationship, background and family of origin. You may also want to ask additional questions about the dysfunctions or problems that have been identified, both in themselves and in their partner. For instance, you'll be interested in whether the problems occur all the time or only in certain situations, such as with this partner but not while masturbating. How it makes them feel about themselves is important to know, as this can contribute to avoidance and anxiety.

The information they give is very important, but so is *the way* they talk about their life. Are they dismissive of events which sound quite painful, suggesting they try to avoid addressing difficult subjects? Do elements of what they say often refute one another? It's inevitable that we'll feel differently at different times, but some people's stories are wildly contradictory. For instance, someone might tell you they orgasm when they want to but at another time refer to difficulties climaxing, perhaps suggesting some shame. In front of their partner, they may say they don't mind that they aren't climaxing, when actually it's very clear that they feel hurt and guilty about this.

This is another reason why seeing the partners individually is so important. There may be subjects they don't wish to discuss in front of each other, even if they're aware of them. They shouldn't be deterred from discussing anything with their therapist for fear that it will be discussed with their partner at some point. It's consequently important to reassure them that their confidence will be respected if they point out no-go aspects of their history; explain how important it is for you to know about the problems.

Conversations in treatment tend to be celebratory and forward looking, but there may be occasions when you need to look back at the problems to evaluate progress or to see whether the partners' attitude has changed. Being clearly non-judgemental from the outset, and appreciating both points of view, will offer considerable reassurance. Replacing questions like, 'Why did you do that?' with, 'What were you hoping for?' sounds less blaming and encourages more consideration. Often a client will answer, 'I don't know, I just panicked!' This provides much more information than 'why' answers which often provoke another question, such as, 'Shouldn't I have?' or defensive responses, such as, 'I knew you'd take their side' or, 'I always do that'. It may also be useful to assess comfort with shared psychoeducation. Some people find this excruciatingly embarrassing or improper. While it's important to improve communication between the couple, there's no point in forcing them into a situation that's so uncomfortable they derive no benefit. For instance, someone with concerns about the appearance of their genitals may profit from seeing photographs or drawings to demonstrate the variety in appearance. However, they may not want to do this in front of their partner or even the therapist, so it can be helpful to organise during the history-taking process rather than once treatment is underway and the couple are being seen together.

Most clients very much enjoy the history taking process, which gives them food for thought, often promoting conversations with their partner and encouraging them to challenge previously fixed ideas. In some cases, this is actually all they need to grow confidence and make effective changes and they don't proceed to, or beyond, the formulation.

FORMULATION

The formulation is the therapist's view of what's been going on as a precursor to treatment. When seeing couples, it's helpful to create a booklet with the same questions opposite each other for partner one and two so these can be compared when compiling the formulation. Often, ideas jump from the pages despite being buried in the clients' narrative and unrecognised until this point.

It's helpful to compile the formulation as a series of headlined bullet points, which encourages a relaxed colloquial style of delivery. Reading out an essay is tempting, but doesn't encourage conversation with the clients and can feel intimidating to them.

THE PROBLEM

It's helpful to start with the clients' view of the problem and what the therapist has also discovered is problematic. In the case of Carla and Hans, mentioned in Chapter 1 (page 13), the therapist noted that Carla and Hans saw their problem as no sexual contact. She had also noted Carla's low libido, coupled with her loss of sexual identity, and Hans' delayed ejaculation.

PRECIPITATING FACTORS: SEX THERAPY

You'll want to clarify what brought the couple to sex therapy. In the case of Carla and Hans, their problems had existed for more than a year, but visiting their GP and her suggestion of sex therapy had made them act.

PRECIPITATING FACTORS: THE PROBLEM

The problem began for Carla when her menopausal symptoms got in the way of sex and made her feel ugly. Hans' difficulties with ejaculating had begun during Carla's pregnancies when he suspected she didn't really want to make love. This improved until Carla's menopausal symptoms when Hans again felt it was inappropriate to make advances and developed difficulties in climaxing.

TRIGGERS

Carla and Hans had almost completely stopped socialising because Carla would start to feel unattractive while getting ready to go out. Carla's low mood and menopausal symptoms triggered Hans' feelings of shame about wanting sex, as he still found her very attractive. They both recoiled from accidental touch, in case the other saw it as a sexual advance, and they then felt guilty.

DISCOURSES AND BELIEFS

It's important to notice the expression of unhelpful ideas which may be maintaining the problems. Sometimes, clients' beliefs are useful, but often they have acquired ideas which aren't helpful at all. Carla felt she had a duty to meet Hans' sexual needs, which she believed were constant in men. Although any form of touch reminded her of how unattractive (she believed) she was, she thought Hans was only unable to ejaculate or want to make love because she was so ugly. She felt ashamed of avoiding sex and of being unattractive. Hans, meanwhile, felt ashamed of wanting sex and finding Carla so attractive. His own mother had been described as 'delicate' and treated with extreme care, and he believed women were fragile and easily hurt. He wholeheartedly believed women stopped enjoying sex during pregnancy and menopause, though in reality some enjoy it more!

MAINTAINING FACTORS

Hans' reluctance to make love and difficulties in climaxing made Carla feel even less sexy, so they both began avoiding physical contact. This was exacerbated by Carla's night time sweating. As this often woke her, she started sleeping in the spare room. Comparing her appearance with her teenage daughters exacerbated her feelings of unloveliness. Getting dressed up to go out used to make Carla feel sexy, but once they stopped socialising – and because dressing up was triggering – there were few enjoyable occasions which might prompt sex. Indeed, their triggers were all maintaining their issues, as were some of their unhelpful beliefs.

POSITIVES

It's important to emphasise the advantages an individual or couple has that contribute to their chance of achieving positive change. The therapist noticed that Carla and Hans spoke warmly and appreciatively about each other and were equally motivated to resolve their sexual issues. They were surprised and delighted to hear this during their formulation meeting, as they'd each assumed the other blamed them for what was happening.

GOALS

While it's important to have clear and measurable goals, a focus on resolving the perceived problem can increase anxiety. Carla and Hans wanted to make love more frequently and for Hans to orgasm more often and sooner. However, when their therapist asked what would make this more likely, they said they would need to feel more relaxed about sex together. The therapist advised making this their overarching goal, as it was likely to contribute to their desired results without undue emphasis on outcomes. She also suggested breaking this main goal down into simple steps, and discussed what they thought would be the first sign of improvement. The couple thought that resuming any form of touch would be a great sign, and this was quickly achieved when the couple began sensate focus experiments.

The history-taking document shouldn't be retired once the formulation has been delivered. It's a valuable resource throughout therapy and can provide new insights from the additional perspective offered by the clients' experience of treatment.

TREATMENT

Treatment can begin after delivering the formulation if the couple still wish to proceed. It's always appropriate to put in place a sex ban at this point to remove pressure, prevent the repetition of old habits and promote safety by treating all touch together as experimental. Touch then becomes a learning experience rather than the kind of win–lose behaviour that's become associated with failure. Whether the therapist continues to allow masturbation depends on how it's being used. If it's an occasional practice which has never interfered with partnered sex, it's usually safe to continue. However, if it's relied on for mood management or is making partnered sex more difficult, work may be needed to develop alternative stress relievers before sex therapy stands any chance of working.

SELF-FOCUS

It's sometimes appropriate to prescribe masturbatory practices, such as the Stop:Start or Wax and Wane experiments described in Chapter 2. Sexual fantasy, erotic reading and guided imagery can be helpful for those with difficulties in reaching orgasm. These may not be introduced immediately, but it's usual to offer self-focus exercises in which individuals mindfully notice their body's reactions to touch and their tolerance to being naked, even when alone. Using a hand mirror to examine the penis from a different angle, or squatting to examine the vulva, can be revelatory, as some people have never properly seen their genitals. Help may be necessary to manage any anxiety or distaste about doing this.

Particularly in those with body image issues, focus is directed to aspects of themselves that clients appreciate. They can also be encouraged to consider their bodies more positively and realistically. For instance, post-pregnancy changes, such as a Caesarean scar or stretch marks, can be framed as inevitable reminders of their amazing achievement in growing a child.

It's helpful to direct clients to notice *negative automatic thoughts* (NATs). Though NATs can arise at any time, they readily occur during sensate focus or when clients think about their bodies. Such thoughts are often self-blaming and harsh, and can maintain sexual difficulties for many reasons including resentment about the need to self-blame! Learning to challenge such thoughts is essential, particularly as it's so easy to imagine that partners share them.

Kegel Exercises involve rapidly tightening and letting go pelvic floor muscles, followed by keeping them clenched for increasing periods of time. The muscles used when halting a stream of urine are the appropriate ones to work. However, stopping mid-stream shouldn't be used in place of Kegels as doing this frequently can cause urinary tract infection. For this reason, it should never be attempted in pregnancy. Kegels are often advised during pregnancy, though, as they strengthen the pelvic floor and help prevent incontinence.

Vaginal clenching can promote orgasm, with some people claiming to orgasm through this method alone. Men can also find Kegels contribute to orgasm, so should not be practised during intercourse for those experiencing early ejaculation. Used regularly, some men claim to experience a more intense orgasm and Kegels are also said to give the penis a more perky appearance as men age.

Many clients benefit from watching short informational films or reading books or articles relevant to their issues. These can provide helpful talking points both within the sessions and between the couple

PRE-SENSATE EXPERIMENTS

Touching exercises between the couple are aimed at encouraging a focus on subjective experience and removing performance and response pressure. Though they should always begin with non-sexual touch, naked touch can be too much for many couples to begin with, especially if they haven't been sexual together for a considerable time. They benefit from starting with less challenging pre-sensate experiments, such as:

- Examining each other's hands in detail, caressing them and, hand over hand, touching their own bodies with them: washing each other's hands can also be used.
- Gazing into each other's eyes without touching whilst lying on separate pillows, noticing any discomfort with this and the way it manifests.
- Fully clothed cuddling or hugging.
- Gently tracing the outline of each other's face with a finger or feather.

This may be the last time for a while that the couple have a con-versation with each other about their likes, as sensate focus requires them to concentrate entirely on their own experience. They're advised to touch one another for their own interest, not to discuss what they're doing and to remain as poker faced as they can. Not knowing how their partner is responding forces couples to stop worrying about the other's response and concentrate on their own. They're advised to experiment with this in pre-sensate exercises, but most people find it extremely difficult and take a while to catch on to what's expected of them. When they do, they find it extremely liberating.

SENSATE FOCUS I

Clients who feel ready to move on from pre-sensate experiments, or who are already comfortable being naked together, are initially offered touching exercises where they explore each other's bodies for their own interest. They're advised that trying not to worry about their partner's pleasure may be the hardest part of this, and that they may need to use mindfulness, self-talk and breathing techniques to manage their anxiety if it occurs.

Planning the experiments is a task in itself. Though couples often insist they'll prioritise the experiments, finding time for them when they're not too tired often turns out to be difficult and sheds light on why they haven't been making love. It's helpful to have them 'book' their first experiments before leaving the therapy session in which they're set, with advice to reschedule immediately if they have to cancel for some reason. Discussing sabotage at this stage makes it less likely, as neither partner usually wishes to be held responsible for therapy not working. A common sabotage is for each partner to wait for the other to initiate the session, so it doesn't happen. This can be avoided by booking the session and giving each partner responsibility for turning up at the appointed time. Though they're told to avoid breasts, buttocks and genitals anyway at this stage, couples with trust or body issues may initially wish to wear a vest and briefs. Sometimes one is okay with being naked, and this needs to be agreed beforehand. Despite there being no expectation of sexual arousal at this stage, it can happen and is worth mentioning in preparation. While some couples are able to ignore an erection, others prefer underpants are worn if this happens.

For the experiment, one partner is designated to choose a location and prepare the area to their own taste. As some couples associate their bedroom with sexual failure, they may want to choose somewhere more relaxing, such as a spare room, sitting room or even a tent in the garden. Though the partner preparing the area is instructed to please themselves, it's worth establishing some rules about this before the event in case one partner has strong feelings about something like heating and doors, windows or curtains being open or shut. Advise soft lighting, though some people can't relax with lights on, at least initially, or can't bear certain smells such as scented candles or incense.

While one partner is preparing the room, the other can have a relaxing bath or shower, perhaps completing some self-focus exercises as well, and can continue this in the room while the other has their shower. They shouldn't comment in any way on how the room has been set up, as negative comments can be sabotaging and even appreciative comments can set up a need to please.

Before beginning, the couple could spend a few moments with the gazing experiment, which is a good way to connect. The partner who prepared the room then spends at least five minutes exploring the other's body with them lying on their stomach, then turning them onto their back to explore the other side and avoiding breasts, buttocks and genitals throughout. They should investigate areas they wouldn't normally look, such as behind the knees and ears, as well as places they already like. Then they swap, and the other partner does the touching. They're advised to have a non-sexual cuddle at the end and not to debrief. The next time they do the experiment the other partner prepares the room.

The first time they try this experiment, they're told to only use dry hands to touch each other, varying pressure and the kind of touch, sometimes using fingertips, sometimes the whole hand. They should be encouraged to notice their reactions to being touched but to try not to discuss this with one another. Then, even when they debrief in therapy, the therapist will try to keep the focus on what they enjoyed doing to the other rather than what they liked being done to them, or didn't like. Much of the conversation will probably be about how they managed feelings of awkwardness or anxiety about the lack of feedback and how they're doing with the self-focus exercises. Any time left over can be used for psychoeducation or work on the relationship.

BLOCKS

The preparation for sensate focus described above anticipates many blocking behaviours before they occur. When they do happen it's usually because one or both partners are highly anxious about something going wrong, being blamed or failing some personal test. Sabotage becomes more likely each time the experiments change or become more challenging. Sometimes only one partner sabotages the experiment, often by making some sort of disparaging comment, but mostly couples collude. One of the most common ways is by breaking the sex ban. This often happens at the beginning of therapy, even when the couple haven't been sexual for years. They are usually aware that it's counterproductive and insist it was 'a last fling'. After this they often settle down. It can be a sign that the couple felt so relaxed and secure with the therapy starting that they found themselves highly aroused and took advantage of this.

Arguing just before an experiment, working late, repeatedly cancelling sessions or reporting that the other partner isn't committed can all be signs of anxiety. It's important to address what's happening. For instance, when exploring ways to make it more likely a couple will attend, some couples may seize the opportunity to say it's not the right time, and quit. It genuinely may not be the right time if they're unable to prioritise therapy. Maybe they're comfortable with what's happening, or maybe they've realised the problem is merely a result of stress and too little time.

Though it may genuinely be the wrong time for couples to invest in their relationship if they're very busy, many remain anxious about the experiments and keep putting them off until just before their next therapy appointment. It's therefore important to address this in the session, emphasising the importance of repeating the experiments as often as they can. This can demonstrate the value of recognising context. These sessions may not go well because they're rushed the night before a therapy appointment or because one or both partners were tired or distracted. So there's often little learning from last minute sensate focus as couples often emerge resentful, sometimes blaming the therapist for setting the task. The therapist needs to reiterate the importance of regular timetabled sessions which are immediately rebooked when missed, and that a major part of the experiment is noticing how they deal with their anxiety about it. They *chose* to enter sex therapy, after considerable explanation and time spent with the therapist. They don't *have* to do this. Gently remind them that this is what they've chosen, sympathising with their anxiety – even when they claim not to have any – and offering support to help overcome it.

Complaining that the experiments are boring, too structured or do nothing for them often happens when clients are full of shame, which they usually discharge towards the therapist who can feel inadequate and unsettled as a result. Patiently explaining again that the experiments aren't meant to be exciting, but that they're a learning experience, often helps. However, some clients are so terrified of failure that they can't accept anything without a clear outcome where they can measure their performance. They will need considerable help to manage their insecurity, sometimes including individual sessions to practise mindfulness, breathing exercises and thought challenging. Catching negative thoughts and noticing changes in bodily sensations can help to alert someone that anxiety is taking over. They can then use their preferred anxiety reduction techniques to reduce the anxiety before it really gets going.

Often, it's the sessions themselves which provide evidence nothing bad will happen, particularly if the clients aren't seeking anxiety provoking outcomes. In fact, the removal of outcome focus usually provides more space for discovery and recognition of what's going well. Partners may, nonetheless, initially express considerable distress about not knowing how the other is finding the experiments. This is to be expected and shouldn't be seen as a block. Developing different attitudes to not knowing, and using them effectively in self-talk, is nearly always necessary.

SENSATE FOCUS PROGRESSION

These initial non-sexual touching experiments can be varied by suggesting use of oils, talcs or body butter (allergies permitting); use of the mouth to blow, lick, suck or kiss; and use of fabrics, feathers, cotton wool or other soft items to touch different body parts. Be sparing with these additions, as some couples need to repeat this experiment several times before they become comfortable with not knowing what the other is thinking and with being touched and being naked. Once they do, and have done this experiment a few times, you can introduce touch of genitals, breasts and buttocks. Couples are still expected to be touching for their own interests, however, and should not try to arouse one another. In practice, though, they often do report feeling aroused. If this is happening to both of them, at least sometimes, they could now take the other's hand in theirs and show them where and how they would like to be touched. This stage shouldn't be introduced until both are able to manage their anxiety and take responsibility for their own experience without feeling threatened by what the other is experiencing. Great care is needed when taking feedback to prevent the return of performance or response anxiety by continuing to focus on individual experience. It's important to emphasise that orgasm is not required, though it's fine if it happens. A conversation about how to manage feelings of frustration following sensate focus allows couples to agree whether they want to masturbate in each other's presence, separately or just let arousal subside. It's vital that they don't ask each other to help out.

By this stage, couples are often expressing considerable satisfaction with the process, feeling much less anxious and closer. The pace of progress should depend on the couple's comfort with it and should continue to begin with room preparation, showers, gazing and non-sexual connection before any sexual touch, and they should still be taking turns. Some self-focus exercises, such as Wax and Wane, Stop:Start or inserting fingers into the vagina, may be introduced into the couple's sessions for the partner to perform once they've been mastered individually.

Variations to sensate focus can now be introduced, such as more kissing or oral sex, but the couple should still be turn-taking rather than engaging in mutual touch. However, at some point couples tend to spontaneously begin mutual touch, often saying it just felt natural at that time. Check that this hasn't caused performance or response pressure – and celebrate. If couples don't begin mutual touch, thoroughly explore how they feel about this before they try it. For those who want to experiment with penetration, encourage genital and digital touch before gentle attempts at intercourse, as described in Chapter 2.

Much of the work once mutual touch has been successfully established is about finessing; finding comfortable positions which maximise pleasure or which promote or delay ejaculation if these are issues. At some point, once they are fully confident, it can be lovely to encourage a further conversation about how they would like to be touched, and how they will manage saying no to sexual advances as well as initiating them. Some couples decide to find regular times for intimacy which may or may not include sex.

ENDING

It's a CBT principle to anticipate the end from the beginning. This can be done with questions about how each partner will know they're progressing. Scaling questions can be used to measure progress. For instance, ask, if zero was the worst things could be, where they feel they are when therapy begins, and ask them to score again as therapy progresses. It's not unusual for couples to feel they've gone backwards at some points when they feel an experiment hasn't gone well. However, these occasions often provide considerable learning, especially when the couple are encouraged to explore what was affecting them. External events may have made relaxed experimentation very difficult, for instance.

Often, it's the couple who feel they've done enough and are ready to go it alone. Because CBT is a stepped process, clients can step off at any point and still have benefited tremendously. For some people, the initial assessment provides such a normalising and informative experience that they already feel changed. History-taking sessions can also promote enough consideration and conversation to result in lasting change. Usually, attending the formulation session as well offers a succinct summary of their learning and an opportunity to discuss the way forward and what would bring them back into therapy. At any point during treatment, the couple may feel empowered to go it alone and should be supported and encouraged to do so. A decision to end shouldn't be seen as therapist failure, but the opposite – the couple have had an enabling experience which has improved their confidence enough to take full control.

Very rarely, a couple will continue to attend therapy even though they appear to have successfully overcome their difficulties. They may still lack confidence and expect their progress will unravel, so it's important to discuss ways to avoid this and how they would recognise it happening.

FOLLOW-UP

It's important to leave the door open for couples to return for therapy if they need to, and it's usual to offer a follow-up session to review how they're getting on. Couples usually enjoy celebrating the way they've maintained their progress. Those with problems often make contact before the follow-up, wondering if they've quit too early. Others are ashamed of not keeping up the momentum, but there are usually good reasons for this which can be helpfully discussed. This eventuality can be anticipated at the final session, and encouragement given to return even for a half-hour appointment where anxieties can often be allayed.

INDIVIDUALS

Therapists working only with individuals may experience a number of limitations. Not seeing the partner means having no idea of the ways they're contributing to the issues through their attitudes or their own unacknowledged problems. It's not ethical to set joint experiments without meeting and knowing the other partner's history, as the experiments may be triggering and they have no support or advice about how to approach them. Despite the drawbacks of individual work, change *is* possible and a good experience may encourage someone back to couple work in future. Much can be done to change attitudes in empowering ways, and the person can experiment with targeted self-focus experiments.

TIME-LIMITED THERAPY

Where individuals or couples have few sessions, it may be necessary to space them further apart and/or to set progressive experiments so they can move on between sessions. Though far from ideal, they may need to complete the history taking online or using a paper questionnaire, using a short call or session to clarify points before the formulation is compiled. This work offers much less opportunity for rapport building, so it may be necessary to create points of communication such as e-mail check-ins or interactive handouts to maintain connection between appointments.

SINGLE SESSION SEX THERAPY

Sometimes clients expect to need only one appointment, especially if they've engaged with television programmes or podcasts where sex or couples therapy happens in a single session. Even when it's unrealistic to expect to fix a longstanding physical problem in an hour, there's often still a great deal that can be achieved. The focus can be changed so that the client(s) emerge from the session feeling considerably more positive and normal. Shame that they haven't known how to fix the issue for themselves, and the feeling that they're different, underpins many relationship and sexual issues, so positive, normalising conversations can be hugely beneficial. A good experience in a single session may be enough to promote change or sustain the couple until they can afford more or move up the NHS waiting list.

The session can be extended by requesting information in advance. As well as briefly describing their problem, clients can be asked what they hope to achieve in the session. This can help identify what will be needed. When they meet, this also allows the therapist to ask whether anything has changed. This simple comparison can lead on to discussion of the skills and resilience being used by the couple and the way external factors can influence the relationship. These are key elements of brief solution-focused therapy, which can be hugely helpful in moving therapy forwards, however many sessions are available. Rapid engagement is promoted by careful listening and, as much as possible, use of the clients' own language which helps them to feel heard and understood.

The focus of the work is on the future, so it's really important to know what the clients want to change rather than allowing them to just offload. It may be necessary to create some boundaries at the beginning to make this clear. Especially if they aren't sure about what they want to change, ask about the effect on their lives because this will reveal what they may want to improve. Even at this early stage, it's worth asking what tiny change would make a difference and how that could happen. Also look for exceptions and times when the problem wasn't around – what made the difference? This may be an external event like being on holiday or the children being on a sleepover. This allows positivity and normalising which, from the start, can be hugely helpful and give clients hope that their problem can shift. Exploring when the problem started may reveal a change in external circumstances which has led to more anxiety, depression or simply less time for intimacy. Comparing any times when they've dealt successfully with *any* problems can reveal strategies and resilience that they hadn't considered or had forgotten, which the therapist can highlight and encourage.

Sometimes, people's beliefs about what they're allowed to do and feel are at odds with what they actually want and need. So it can be helpful to investigate how they acquired these ideas. It can also be useful to ask when they last had a *new* idea about what's possible and what it would be like if they could think more freely.

PERSONAL CONSENT

It can be helpful to suggest a personal consent check-in to look at the way their life is and whether this is what they want. Where do sex and intimacy fit and what small change would be helpful to make it all work better? It's easy to slide into ways of thinking and behaviours that aren't comfortable but which we feel can't be changed. Often, they can be made easier or even abandoned. Couples can do this together, even using part of the session to get started, or separately before comparing their findings.

THE MIRACLE QUESTION

Miracle questions ask the clients to imagine that overnight a miracle occurs whereby their problem is resolved, but they don't know it's happened because they were sleeping when it took place. Asking what tiny sign they would notice when they woke up that would tell them things had changed can produce profound results. Therapists often have difficulty with this sort of question, however, if they allow a focus on major change. Keeping the focus on small changes tends to have more dramatic results, as the possibilities being explored seem more likely. Ask, for example, what they would feel when they opened their eyes following the miracle? What would be the first thing they would do? Couples often say they'd be in bed together and/or that they'd be touching or would roll over for a cuddle, something that may not have happened for a while. Another sign that things have changed may be something as simple as smelling their partner making coffee for breakfast, if they hadn't started their day in this way for a while.

Solution focus specialist Mark McKergow recommends making the miracle question as elaborate as possible, using what's known about clients' routines to help them tune in to the question. So, in setting up the question, the therapist might discuss what will happen when the couple leave the session. Maybe they'll go back to work, collect children from school, prepare an evening meal, take charge of bath time, watch some television before going to bed. Maybe they'll feel sad when they roll over to different sides of the bed or retire to different rooms without a kiss ….

Therapists often over-complicate the miracle question in their own heads, assuming clients will find it too difficult to answer. But if you've just been discussing what they want to change, they're often able to elaborate this with little or no prompting. If they say they don't know what will be different, you could remind them of what they told you about how the problem is affecting their lives. What would it be like if that changed? Scaling how distressing the problem is now – with zero being the worst possible distress and 10 being the least – and comparing this with where it would be after the miracle, often reveals that couples would settle for much less than perfect. For instance, someone who has had radical prostate surgery may wish for an immediate return of erections, but would like to be allowed to make love and give their partner pleasure. Perhaps both partners would adore this but have avoided sex, fearing erectile difficulties would upset the other.

At the end of a session where possibilities and differences have been revealed, most clients leave with a number of resolutions and a vastly improved sense of hope.

SYSTEMIC THERAPY

Brief solution-focused therapy is one version of **systemic therapy**, which is really an umbrella term for approaches which explore how contexts beyond the individual affect them. It's interested in how systems function, interact and are affected by other contexts and systems. So, for instance, a therapist looking beyond a couple system would be interested in how that system gets along with each of the wider family systems and, beyond these, systems and contexts such as their friendship groups, working life, religion, ethnic heritage, education, culture, finances and so on … The Social Grraaaccceeessss described on page 52 offer a way of exploring how different contexts intersect.

Systemic therapists explore using the language of difference and comparison, often employing specific kinds of question which challenge the listener. For instance, there are many ways to ask questions about sex losing its spice:

- Was sex more boring before or after your baby arrived?
- Before you moved in together, was sex more spontaneous?
- In the future, which of you is likely to be the more sexually adventurous?
- Was sex more creative when you were first together?
- What small change to your sexual routine would make a big difference?
- Which of you is more likely to do something different?
- What is Y most likely to do to initiate sex?
- When X initiates, what do you do? And how does X respond?
- Y, what do you think X will do if things don't improve?

Therapists are slow to understand, asking many clarifying questions to ensure they've understood and to deepen clients' own understanding. Many couples have no curiosity about one another's motivation or meaning, believing their assumptions to be truths. Most of the time, they completely misunderstanding each other, so the therapist's modelling of curiosity, and the new information it reveals, can transform a couple's insight.

Genograms, or family maps, may be used to explore the different relationships and beliefs of family members, which can also reveal why partners misunderstand each other. They're useful for general exploration but also for exploring specific concepts such as sexuality. It can be especially helpful to ask about family members' mottos which often reveal ideas which are influencing the partners generally and sexually. For instance, mottos in one partner's family may be exceptionally permissive, such as 'Make hay while the sun shines' or 'Love the one you're with', while the other's may be less liberal, such as, 'Don't appear interested in sex' or 'Keep sex for one special person'. The motto or message to 'Be happy' superficially appears positive and helpful. However, it's an instruction that can be oppressive. Someone who has grown up in a household which discouraged the expression of negativity may have no idea how to manage less than positive feelings or circumstances, let alone how to explain them to their partner. Similarly, the instruction to be happy can create a sense of failure when someone is going through a stressed or low period or just doesn't feel full of beans. When there's no acknowledgement in a family that ups and downs are normal, and little help to cope with this, many people believe that relationships shouldn't require effort, and that there's something wrong if sex isn't perfect.

The way clients' families treated bodies can be very helpful to know too. 'Banter' about sexual development, weight or appearance can cause lasting self-consciousness, and rough handling or strict control of appearance can lead to low sexual confidence. Genograms may also reveal family pride in some contexts, but shame in others. For instance, Gloria's family was proud of having beautiful black skin and attractive bodies, but ashamed when women in the family made the most of this or dressed in ways they saw as provocative. Older family members saw this as encouraging a racial stereotype of black sexuality they didn't think applied to them.

SOCIAL CONSTRUCTIONISM

Taking a curious stance as to how we reach conclusions about our world reveals that what we accept as 'normal' or 'true' isn't a natural or innate quality of a thought, situation or behaviour but has been socially constructed by people. It follows that being curious about how people develop their ideas can reveal discomfort with them but a belief that this is the 'right' way to be and that there are no alternatives. Exploring this in sex therapy can make a tremendous difference. For instance, many people believe there is one true love they need to find, a soulmate who can fulfil all their needs. However, this idea is recent. In most of the world and for most of history, couples have paired on the basis of convenience; love may, or may not, have come later. Living in traditional families is good for the economy, as the need to provide for a wife and children provides a workforce and, of course, a provider. Feeding the idea of The One also keeps families together and less of a drain on the state. The promotion of families with children is also a reason to outlaw gay and non-binary relationships which have historically been seen as less likely to include children. This is discussed further in Chapter 4.

A critique of social constructionism is that it ignores scientific 'fact', such as biological sex. However, if you see social constructionism as a way of exploring the world rather than itself a 'truth', it's much easier to see how it helps to allow what works for people rather than imposing social ideas which are pragmatic and changeable. Permitting difference in this way has allowed for non-binary sexualities, polyamory and asexuality, for example.

FEMINIST THERAPIES

Developed in the 1960s and 1970s, as a response to male domination of psychotherapy, feminist therapies exist as a discipline in their own right, whilst sharing many elements of systemic therapy and adopting a social constructionist stance. Far from seeing problems as located in the individual, feminist therapies see individuals' issues as responses to their environment, and to oppression in particular. This means paying attention to power differentials, including those which exist in the relationship with the therapist, who will take seriously the client's version of their experiences and avoid interpretation. There's recently been more attention paid to *intersectionality* – or how contexts interact – too, making this an appropriate way of working with everyone, not just women (see also page 138). However, women and other marginalised groups benefit particularly from exploration of themselves and their oppressed groups in relation to the world.

In sex therapy, it's enormously helpful to explore how **discourses** around sex and gender are acquired and how they're affecting the couple's lives. Women may also have experiences which have influenced their expectations, and may especially have learned to feel their bodies or minds are dysfunctional or not fully their own. For instance, thinking he was being supportive, Klaus told Amelia she should have more confidence at work and that she was probably imagining the put-downs she was experiencing from male colleagues. Their therapist pointed out that Klaus had never himself experienced being a woman in a work environment, urging him to notice how women were treated in his own workplace. Similarly, Gary told Helen her self-consciousness about her weight was 'silly' as he loved her and found her attractive. Their therapist noted that women are bombarded with media messages about weight and attraction, and that Helen's own family had valued slimness. As they explored this, Helen became aware of her belief that Gary cared for her in spite of her weight, not that it didn't matter to him. His dismissal of her distress meant she was unable to feel sexual or comfortably express her sexuality, so that she had retreated into the protection of low desire.

Obviously, many – if not all – women will have experienced unwanted sexual attention at some point in their lives, which may be affecting the way they relate to their partners. Some may feel triggered by unwelcome touch from their partner or hurtful 'teasing', particularly about their bodies. Many partners also fall into gendered roles which are unhelpful to the relationship, even when they're well-meaning. For instance, Maraid had been brought up around people who believed women should be available for sex and were responsible for the emotional temperature of the relationship. She consequently responded with shame and appeasement when her partner told her she wasn't trying hard enough. Talking to her therapist about the way he treated her led to a realisation that her partner was making no effort and that the relationship was abusive.

EXTERNALISING

Externalising interventions encourage couples to consider their problems as outside themselves. For instance, someone with low libido can be encouraged to describe this as if it's an entity beyond them with a mind of its own. Listening for what the client calls this can begin the process. Alternatively you can choose a name – 'Low Spice?' – and just start using it, or even ask the client to pick a name. Ask them what it would look like if it could be seen, when it's around, what it says to them and why they think it wants to be so troublesome. Externalising can be used with almost anything, including arguing or troublesome sexual dynamics, but should be avoided when addressing any form of power dynamics or abuse, which needs to be tackled directly.

PARTS THERAPIES

It's fairly easy to accept that we all behave in different ways in different circumstances and with different people. Sometimes, though, those ways don't appear to be under conscious control and we actually dissociate so that the active, aware, here-and-now part of our brain goes offline and we're hijacked by memory parts. These are essentially defences, developed at different stages in our lives, to protect the young vulnerable parts of ourselves. Different theorists see these parts in different ways, but all agree they are developed to be protective. However, parts aren't all in agreement and can get in the way of normal life. For instance, it's common when growing close to another person to develop sexual problems, such as erectile difficulties or low libido, or behaviours which damage the relationship, such as flirting with someone else, staying out late or even affairs. When asked why they do this, many people don't know – often, a part is trying to protect them from becoming too close to someone else, and thereby risking hurt or rejection.

This can be worked with simply as an elaboration of externalising by discussing when the part is around and what it wants. Many clients enthusiastically explore their sexual versus sexually avoidant parts, increasingly taking control. This is because it's impossible to imagine the parts whilst hijacked by them, so the more someone describes, explores and talks to a part, the more they are engaging their here-and-now brain. Gradually, they incorporate parts so they can use them consciously rather than finding they take over.

INTERNAL FAMILY SYSTEMS (IFS)

IFS therapy, developed by family therapist Richard Schwartz, is one increasingly popular way of working with parts, particularly when the parts are very active and difficult for someone to connect with. Schwartz described the parts as 'managers', 'firefighters' and 'exiles'. It's the managers' and firefighters' job to protect the exiles, which are young and vulnerable parts, from connecting the person with distressing experiences of abuse, neglect or pain.

MANAGERS

Manager parts can give the impression that someone is well-functioning, because they impose rules and ways of behaving that create safety for the person. However, these can be restrictive and black and white in outlook, limiting someone's options and closing down curiosity. They can affect all aspects of life, including sexual expression, perhaps controlling what touch is allowed or whether it's okay to orgasm. The part may believe orgasm would make them out of control or vulnerable or that 'giving' this to their partner is dangerous. Nonetheless, the person experiencing this may be highly frustrated or distressed by their inability to orgasm and assume there's a medical reason why they aren't climaxing.

FIREFIGHTERS

When a threat feels more urgent, reactive firefighter parts may cause a person to act apparently impulsively and, perhaps, problematically. For instance, rather than managing feelings of distress or boredom, they may seek distraction through pornography, alcohol, drugs or another relationship. To avoid the risks associated with becoming close to someone, they may start an argument or lose their erection. Partners' own protective parts may respond to defend their own vulnerabilities, so that couples can easily become locked into toxic patterns where they repeatedly experience crisis each time they risk becoming closer. It's no coincidence that couples often present with a recent catastrophe around the time of some sort of commitment, such as becoming engaged, moving in, marrying, buying a bigger house or becoming pregnant.

EXILES

Not until someone becomes aware of their manager and firefighter parts, and how they're functioning, are they able to separate from them and reach their exiled parts. Couples can be encouraged to notice how they're behaving, thinking and feeling, and what's going on in their bodies, at different times. The more they elaborate the parts, the more it becomes possible to thank them for their support, but ask them to step aside so that the exiles can be reached. Sometimes it's possible for the therapist to speak directly with an exile or, more often, for the client to speak with them, tell their story and start processing their pain. It can be illuminating for clients to ask protectors how old they are and how old they think the client is. It's common for protectors to be children or adolescents and to think the client is still a child who is often younger than themselves. Most protectors and all exiles are consequently unaware that the difficult experiences they had are no longer ongoing, so they can be considerably reassured by their connection with the adult self. It's the hidden presence of exiles which ultimately makes couples treat each other as if they pose a threat, and why it's so difficult to interrupt this.

When each partner understands what's going on for them, they're enabled to work with their own behaviours and vulnerabilities rather than trying to change each other, often discovering how similar they are. IFS encourages each partner to unblend from protective parts and to instead employ positive attributes of the here-and-now self, which include:

- Curiosity
- Calm
- Connectedness
- Clarity
- Confidence
- Compassion
- Courage
- Creativity.

Partners are often able to notice when they're using these and when parts are around. This enables them to be aware of, and take responsibility for, their own part in their relationship dynamic. They may then be able to 'stand down' protective parts, reassure exiles and reclaim their sexual selves. For some people, though, this can be a difficult process, and they may benefit from more specialist parts work or EMDR (see page 175) to directly address their fears and trauma. In some therapies, clients can visualise their young and vulnerable exiles and rescue them from the dangers they experienced by sending in their here-and-now selves to take charge. Unless they've had additional trauma training, most sex therapists would refer for specialist work, but may be able to continue sex therapy with caution.

PSYCHODYNAMIC APPROACHES

An understanding of psychodynamic theory is enormously helpful when working with relationships. In particular, the concepts of defences, transference and projection can illuminate what underlies an unhelpful couple dynamic. Couples always join relationships with unconscious expectations and hopes about what will happen, as well as the psychological consequences of their experiences with previous partners. Therapists, too, have ideas about relationships based on what happened in their own families, current relationships and the experiences of their clients.

Transference occurs when someone unconsciously treats another person as if they were someone from their past. For instance, if they've had a critical father their expectation of others may be that they will judge them and criticise. Close relationships and therapy particularly trigger old feelings, and we often hear partners exclaiming, 'I'm not your mother!'.

It's possible to pick up the transference and project back a personal reaction, something that is known to happen in therapy (countertransference). This is one reason why it's so useful for us to have our own therapy and to develop a reflexive approach to our work, so that we can work out what's happening when we have strong reactions to our clients (see pages 88 and 165–166).

Towards the end of treatment, therapists sometimes find themselves being asked about, or offering, some sort of personal detail. This is a sign that the transference is loosening and they are becoming more real to the client.

COUPLE FIT

Though we're aware of physical allure, social suitability and common beliefs and interests, most of us don't realise that powerful unconscious attraction draws us to particular partners. Without this, relationships would be short-lived as there would be nothing to keep us involved beyond the initial relaxed and uncritical honeymoon period. We're often initially attracted to someone who seems completely unlike, say, a critical and overbearing parent with whom we had a difficult and unsatisfying relationship. However, once into the relationship we may find this idyllic partner shares many of that parent's attributes. The unconscious need to get the relationship right this time can then help us to resolve the issues that developed as a result of the relationship with that parent. Alternatively, the relationship with the 'familiar' partner can become anti-developmental, keeping us locked into unhappy or toxic relationships forever. Recognising what we're playing out can help us to manage what's happening and separate really unacceptable behaviours from triggers and transference. We also need to recognise how our own behaviour provokes familiar, if unpleasant, responses from our partner so that we can better control a conflictual or hurtful dynamic.

Couple fit isn't always dramatic or painful. The more partners are able to take responsibility for their own feelings and actions, the more they can use the relationship effectively to learn and grow. Sometimes they outgrow what the relationship has to offer and need to move on to another relationship with different potential. This should be seen as an extremely successful relationship rather than one that failed. Indeed, when both partners reach this stage at around the same time, they're often able to end amicably and remain great friends. However, many relationships are dominated by defences acquired over a lifetime and the couple re-enact their early relationships rather than being able to develop.

IMAGO

Imago refers to the unconscious image we have of how our ideal lover will be, incorporating the relationships we've seen and hoped for as well as aspects of the relationships we had with our caregivers. The purpose of our important adult relationships is to improve on these. The therapy, originally developed by Harville Hendrix, is interested in the way couples relate and how they protect their individual vulnerabilities. It works with the hurt and disappointment couples feel once the honeymoon period has ended, helping each partner to recognise that their unmet needs in the relationship are the same as their unmet needs in childhood. This may assist couples to appreciate and take responsibility for their own part of the relationship dynamic, especially as they may immediately feel more understood and validated. Nonetheless, self-validation is needed if unhelpful projecting and conflict are to be stopped. A first step may be to help each partner recognise internalised messages which are organising their thinking and behaviour. Instead of treating each other as if they're making these demands, they're helped to notice these messages and decide whether to continue obeying them or to create new ideas. This is especially helpful in sex therapy where messages acquired earlier in life may be highly inhibiting or create rules which someone's partner is unaware of. Once this is recognised, each partner can develop an active and conscious approach to their sexual expression.

Of course, treating the conflict between couples is necessary to allow space for such personal exploration. Imago sees couples' coping mechanisms as occurring in external 'energy-out' behaviours, such as blaming or bickering, and 'energy-in' behaviours, such as shut-down or stonewalling. They're helped to develop a collaborative stance in which they can acknowledge their difference whilst being on the same side. Part of this is the acquisition of listening skills and participation in highly structured conversations where they learn how to respond appreciatively and empathically.

TRANSACTIONAL ANALYSIS (TA)

TA is also interested in the behaviour between couples which it recognises as being played out in a series of 'games' which serve to continue a couple's unhelpful dynamic. A feature of the game is that the couple ignore information which could produce a resolution of their problem, and instead keep repeating the same old moves. This can be because each partner is relating to their own life scripts and messages rather than paying attention to their present context and the other partner. Once couples are aware of the games, they have the opportunity to change them.

TA pays great attention to couples' needs – referred to as 'hungers' – including their sexual needs and how these are expressed and welcomed. Sexual games are common (pursuer:distancer games are an example), but even these are enactments of much earlier relationship dynamics, usually arising in the family of origin. Couples are helped to change collusive behaviours by recognising their origins and staying as much as possible within their adult selves so that critical projections and childish responses are avoided.

ATTACHMENT

Finding existing psychoanalytic theories inadequate, psychologist and psychiatrist John Bowlby developed a theory of attachment which explored how early relationships influence a child's development and potential to form secure and meaningful adult relationships. Bowlby was brought up by nannies and sent to boarding school aged seven, rarely seeing his parents. The departure of his favourite nanny was a blow from which he never recovered, and led him to research the way relationships affect development throughout life. He noted that the way children are treated influences their expectations about the world. This set of expectations is known as an *Internal Working Model* which plays out in the way people react to others. For instance, if they expect to be dismissed and criticised, they may perceive rejection and censure when it's not actually what someone's intending to convey at all. They may also have more difficulty trusting others, particularly as relationships become closer.

Psychologist Mary Ainsworth devised the Strange Situation Experiment, which enabled her to recognise the developing attachment styles of children aged from nine to 17 months in relation to their main caregiver, usually their mother. By observing their behaviour when left with an unfamiliar adult, and their reaction to their mother on her return, she noted three main attachment behaviours:

A – These children pay little attention to their caregiver or the stranger and may appear absorbed in their play. Because they seem so unperturbed, they can be confused with securely attached children (B). However, they may be hiding distress and anxiety. This behaviour arises when their caregiver failed to validate their emotions or help them manage their feelings. Indeed, they may have been taught not to show emotion, and experience considerable shame about doing so, making them reluctant to join therapy.

They often give short unelaborated answers in history taking, insisting their childhood was 'normal' or 'unexceptional', though they will usually describe their mother as exceptionally wonderful. However, they can rarely remember much about their childhood or offer examples to demonstrate their mother's wonderfulness or their childhood's ordinariness.

Though often appearing outwardly confident, they may be unsure that relationships will survive closeness or that they will survive scrutiny. They can consequently seem assured, thoughtful and enthusiastic lovers initially, but often avoid sex once the relationship becomes closer. Partners often complain that they won't discuss their feelings and that they're unsupportive. Because they're uncomfortable with the expression of emotion, they tend to develop physical rather than emotional signs of distress, including sexual dysfunctions.

B – In the Strange Situation Experiment, securely attached children may show distress when their caregiver leaves but be soothed by the stranger and pleased to see their caregiver when they return. They have a positive Internal Working Model, and are able to have trusting, long-term relationships in which they can readily give and receive support, express feelings and needs and be comfortable with intimacy.

C – Children are distressed both when the caregiver leaves and when they return, and are unsoothed by the stranger. They will already have experienced inconsistent and unboundaried parenting, and may later be made to feel responsible for the feelings and experience of their caregiver. This means they can be over-intrusive adults. They see themselves as empathic listeners and supportive friends, but are often disappointed by others' care of them. This can make them anxious and demanding in relationships, finding it impossible to walk away or calm down when triggered. Difficulty **mentalizing** means they may misread others' intentions and react in ways that push people away. They may cling to hopeless relationships, despite being angry and critical of them. Though they desperately want to be in a relationship, and may attach quickly, their Internal Working Model makes it difficult to be close. They may be comfortable with relationships becoming sexual quickly, but misread their lovers' intentions, and become upset when relationships don't progress.

These A–C attachment behaviours were later named avoidant/ dismissing (A), secure (B) and ambivalent/preoccupied (C) by Mary Main who also added D, which she called 'disorganised/dis- oriented-fearful' and which may be associated with considerable neglect or abuse. A noticeable feature of D children in the Strange Situation Experiment is that they may run towards the caregiver on their return but then freeze and drop to the floor, as they recall that the source of their comfort is also the cause of their pain. While people with A and C attachments may not be con- sciously aware of difficulties with intimacy, Ds *are* aware of expecting rejection and hurt, often actively avoiding intimacy. They may consequently be extremely controlling in relationships, either by becoming intensely solicitous and caring or rejecting and cruel. Sexual relationships can trigger the confusing feelings associated with early relationships so that couples often present with a history of long-term **dissociation**, relationship and sexual problems.

Further attachment assessments have been developed for other age groups than infancy, including one for adults, which applies to relationships generally, not just the way people relate to their pri- mary childhood caregiver. Though few sex and relationship therapists have received the intensive training necessary to code attachment styles, a broad knowledge of their features can be extremely helpful. It can, for instance, be seen that insecurely attached adults have reason to unconsciously collude in ways which sabotage closeness.

MENTALIZING

Cs and Ds often have poor theory of mind which makes it difficult for them to be curious about others' point of view or think about their own thinking, both essential for effective mentalizing. Indeed, it could be argued that parents with good mentalizing capacity produce the most securely attached children, who are able to reason and self-soothe with confidence. Though some Ds in particular may exhibit grandiose and over-confident behaviours, these are essentially fake and developed to hide from themselves their extreme shame and confusion. Flipping between different mood states, or parts, makes it difficult for Ds to understand their own motivation, let alone explain it to their partners, and they often respond to questions about this with answers such as, 'It's obvious', 'You know very well' or 'If you don't know, I won't tell you'. Because they have difficulty reading others too, and are so sensitive, it can be helpful to ask lots of mindreading questions about the other partner in their presence, so they can experience the therapist mentalizing in conversation with them.

MENTALIZING CONFLICT

At least one partner in couples experiencing toxic conflict will have mentalizing difficulties, which often disrupt the other's attachment security too as their thought processes can be so hard to fathom and manage. This can be because they conflate thoughts with events in the real world, a process known as *psychic equivalence*. For instance, someone hoping their partner will, say, buy them flowers may be furious when they don't, even though the partner had no clue this was expected.

Despite framing sex therapy exercises as experimental, such clients are often negative about their progress, often being highly critical of their partner's role despite the therapist's insistence on appreciative comment only. Engaging with content is rarely helpful, and arguing is always counterproductive, but asking someone how they're coping with the issues they express can promote mentalizing. They may ultimately notice that they're unable to provide answers about their motivation and experience, whereas the therapist and their partner can. Thus, they gradually gain confidence in self-exploration and begin replacing meaningless and lengthy pseudo-intellectualising with genuine reflection.

EMOTIONALLY FOCUSED THERAPY (EFT)

This process is also a feature of EFT which works well with the many couples who exhibit a dynamic through which they unconsciously collude to defend themselves and avoid change through the exchange of unconscious *projections*. In a pursuer:distancer dynamic, for example, which is commonly seen between A and C couples, one partner may enthusiastically pursue their more reluctant partner for sex, only to withdraw when the partner starts to initiate sex themselves. EFT seeks to gently expose the underlying vulnerabilities of the dynamic, allowing each partner to own and express them rather than hide them beneath the conveyed emotion, which is often anger. Their eventual ability to explore their needs with confidence in a, by then, much safer relational environment, reduces the need for their formerly toxic relating and helps heal attachment wounds.

> An unromantic aspect of relationships is that we select partners who may assist our self-development and who will respond to our *projections*. These occur when unwanted aspects of the self are unconsciously split off and attributed to someone else. For instance, we may accuse someone else of being angry when it's actually us that is seething. *Projective identification* occurs when someone responds to these attributions, often attempting to defend themselves from the projection.
>
> Projective identification is extremely common between couples, and accounts for a great deal of their conflict. For instance, one partner may say the other is lazy when they're actually not at all hard working themselves. The outraged and upset other may then protest but feel unable to relax in case the accusation is levelled at them again.

Typically, couples have contributed to each other's attachment injuries through specific incidents and ongoing failure to meet each other's needs. This hurt and disappointment is specifically targeted in EFT, revealing each partner's intentions and regrets about what's happened between them. However, the focus of the work is on changing the distressing couple dynamic and expressing hurt and need more honestly and appropriately. This is done in a staged and structured way, where the content of the couple's complaints is seen as a reflection of the underlying feelings and attachment profile.

OTHER APPROACHES

SEXUAL CRUCIBLE

Psychologist Dr David Schnarch believed that most couples find sex boring because they try so hard to please one another and eliminate any difference between them. Most people's aim, he said, is to receive validation from their partner, so they exclude risk and sex becomes dull and predictable. But partners are bound to have different sexual appetites and interests. Rather than ignoring these, each partner should be prepared to explore and negotiate with the other, Schnarch insisted.

He didn't believe in sex therapy exercises like sensate focus or in communication coaching. Instead, he felt each partner should learn to manage their anxiety and self-validate, so that they would have confidence to express their sexuality in the way they really wanted to. They wouldn't always agree, and their differences may be a deal breaker, but their ability to self-validate would offer much more scope for discovery and reflection. Schnarch advocated modelling this by naming the unsaid and getting to the heart of a couple's issues as they appear to the therapist.

Despite his evident dislike of sex therapy experiments, he did suggest consciousness-raising exercises which promote self-advocacy such as 'hugging 'til relaxed' while 'standing on your own two feet', gazing at each other with heads on separate pillows and keeping eyes open during sex.

WHEEL OF CONSENT

Somatic sex educator Dr Betty Martin's Wheel of Consent helps people to check in with themselves and each other to work out what's happening for them in any sexual interaction. Many couples find themselves in sexual situations which neither of them may be enjoying or wanting, or where one feels exploited. However, it may not even occur to them that this could be different or that having the touch/sex/communication they want could make their relationship richer and more fulfilling. The Wheel of Consent can be used to awake people to their sexual potential, so that they become more aware of their bodies and what they can do, and also to help them recognise what their minds are doing when they involve themselves in a sexual transaction.

The four elements of the wheel are:

Giving
Taking
Allowing
Receiving

On the face of it, these seem completely straightforward actions, but they're all much more nuanced than it would first appear. In a sexual encounter, the wants and needs of the couple may not coincide. Schnarch is very aware of this, of course, and keen for couples to realise that their differences are okay. For instance, many people assume they're giving when they're actually allowing. Letting your partner touch you can be seen as a gift, but it may be done because someone feels obligated or coerced rather than because they willingly allow, so allowing doesn't always imply autonomous consent or pleasure.

Many people find it difficult to ask for what they want, making sex remarkably hit and miss, with both partners guessing what the other wants and possibly feeling disappointed with what they get or too focused on what they think the other wants to really experience pleasure. Martin uses The Three Minute Game, developed by Harry Faddis, a life coach for gay men, to help couples explore this. Basically, the game involves couples asking each other how they want to touch and be touched for three minutes, noticing how it feels to ask and be asked. When someone realises they can't agree to requested touch in a wholeheartedly positive way, they are encouraged not to agree. It's also important to know that people can change their minds about what they want, even while something they originally agreed to is happening.

Familiarity with the game helps partners both consider what they want and learn to ask, take and refuse comfortably. This is of enormous benefit in sex therapy, particularly for couples who are outcome driven.

THE GOOD ENOUGH SEX MODEL

Sexologists Michael Metz and Barry McCarthy developed the Good Enough Sex Model to encourage couples to appreciate that there's no one-size-fits-all approach to lovemaking. Attempting to remove pressure from sex, they urge couples to resist a focus on outcomes and to explore what works best for them, ignoring all the hype around frequency and requirements for phenomenal, perfect experiences. This view is now so widely accepted that it can be expected in all modern sex therapy.

THE DUAL CONTROL MODEL

Clients may already be aware of the Dual Control Model, as it appears in women's sexuality lecturer Emily Nagoski's best selling book, *Come As You Are*. Originally introduced by sex researchers Dr John Bancroft and Dr Erick Janssen, it focuses on what turns people on and off sex – which Nagoski refers to as 'accelerators' and 'brakes'. As with the Good Enough Sex Model, Bancroft and Janssen recognised that sexual response is a highly individual process and that physiological arousal may go unnoticed if there are sufficient brakes to distract the person. These tend to be distracting thoughts associated with performance anxiety. This suggests that many people may think they have an arousal or desire problem when, in fact, their desire or arousal is there but is being suppressed by their anxiety. Mood and context also have a role in whether an individual notices sexual cues and responses. Interestingly, depression can actually lead to increased sexual risk taking, maybe as a way of 'experiencing' when the depression has left them feeling numb. Other forms of risk taking, such as extreme sport, have long been associated with traumatic numbness, for instance.

Janssen and Bancroft developed questionnaires to explore people's experience of accelerators and brakes – the Sexual Inhibition (SIS) and Sexual Excitation (SES) Scales – but it may be possible for clients to start recognising brakes and accelerators by themselves or in therapy. Comparing times when sex was satisfying, or arousal was easy, with more recent experiences may offer clues about the situations and thoughts which prompt the brakes to go on or promote sexual interest. Explaining that there's much more to sexual response than just providing the right physical stimulation can also provide considerable reassurance.

SEXUAL GROUNDING THERAPY (SGT)

Based on the work of Willem Poppeliers, Sexual Grounding Therapy explores the way relationships develop and sex is expressed and influenced throughout the lifespan. Babies, for instance, require caregivers to reflect their experience and interpret the world for them. But when the infants are required to do the soothing, they may become adults who focus on managing the experience of the other rather than being able to focus on themselves. Indeed, this mirroring of their experience is absent from the lives of many people whose sexual development was not welcomed or was treated inappropriately. Examples include distracting or chiding children when they explore their own bodies or teasing adolescents about the changes associated with puberty. Moreover, according to SGT, there may be little evidence of one's parents as sexual beings, which closes down the natural sexual energy and curiosity in us.

Therapy is offered in experiential groups focused on changing sexual scripts through body work and giving people a sense of having parents who support and celebrate their sexual maturation. This work is very different from traditional sex therapy, and is either misunderstood or controversial depending on your viewpoint. Nonetheless, there is much that is familiar in terms of helping people discover a different way of approaching their sexual selves and potential.

MEDICAL MODEL

Many people don't appreciate the link between general health, sex and reproduction and may appreciate referral to, say, a dietitian or personal trainer to discuss healthier lifestyle choices. Some clients have been struggling for a considerable time with undiagnosed or unresolved physical issues which affect their self-image and sexual functioning and may need support to persist in seeking clinical solutions. It's also important not to assume sexual problems are entirely psychological and to rule out physical contributions. As more medical professionals become interested in maintaining and restoring sexual health, so more will be performing a sex therapy function as well as working with and referring to fully qualified sex therapists.

HOLISTIC APPROACH

Doctors, nurses and physiotherapists all work with issues affecting sexual functioning, often as part of a multidisciplinary team. While many will examine, run tests, diagnose, prescribe and refer, there are sex therapists who also take a largely 'medical' approach. A feature of these is sometimes that treatment ends when there is an improvement in the presented problem rather than seeking and treating associated psychological issues. Some take an holistic approach, looking at diet, exercise and lifestyle habits such as alcohol intake, smoking and use of recreational drugs and prescribed medication.

MEDICATION

Many couples expect a pharmacological solution to their sexual problems now that sildenafil (Viagra) is available over the counter. It's one of a number of **PDE 5 inhibitors** – also discussed on page 26 – which improve blood supply to the penis, facilitating erection. However, sexual interest and stimulation are also required, and sildenafil doesn't suit everyone. Issues with timing can cause inhibiting anxiety, for instance. It has to be taken half an hour before sex and the effects last about two hours. The effects of tadalafil (Cialis), in particular, and vardenafil (Levitra) can last longer but for most people are only available with a private prescription, which some couples find surprising and which brings them to sex therapy as an alternative. They are contraindicated with some conditions, including low blood pressure and some other cardiovascular conditions, such as strokes. Some people experience unpleasant side effects, particularly a blocked or runny nose and indigestion.

PRESCRIBED DRUGS

It's helpful for sex therapists to be familiar with prescribed medication and able to discuss it with clients, as some drugs interfere with sex. For example, hormonal contraceptives can cause low desire, vaginal dryness and painful sex. Leuprorelin (Leupron), which is used to treat hormone dependent cancers, other conditions involving hormones such as endometriosis and fibroids, and can be used to delay puberty, may have a direct effect on sexual functioning. Loss of desire and ED are direct effects, and indirect effects include night sweats and hot flushes, tiredness, joint pain and breast tenderness.

Drugs for cardiovascular conditions also have both direct and indirect effects on sex. Statins can reduce testosterone and cause loss of desire and ED. Beta blockers also affect desire and cause ED, as well as causing tiredness, tummy upsets and depression. Thiazide diuretics can cause ED and delayed ejaculation.

Medication to treat mental health conditions has also been implicated. Anti-psychotic drugs can cause low desire, arousal and erection difficulties, anorgasmia and delayed ejaculation, plus bed wetting, fatigue, headache and weight gain. Tricyclic and tetra-cyclic antidepressants have been implicated in delayed orgasm and low desire. Selective serotonin uptake inhibitors (SSRIs) are more commonly prescribed antidepressants which can cause ED, reduced vaginal lubrication, anorgasmia and delayed ejaculation.

RECREATIONAL DRUGS

Most clients are aware that alcohol can cause erectile issues in men and orgasm difficulty in women but may not know it can lower testosterone, as can tobacco use. Amphetamines, cannabis, cocaine, GHB, ketamine, MDMA, methadone and heroin can cause ED and orgasm difficulties. Cocaine initially increases desire but within a year of regular use it can lead to loss of desire, ED and orgasm problems. Cannabis can cause orgasm difficulties and dyspareunia.

CULTURAL ADJUSTMENT

Sometimes the attitudes and approaches of sex therapy conflict with the cultural or religious requirements of our clients. Mas-turbation may be prohibited, for example. It is, however, worth checking this with a couple's religious advisers, as this rule can often be amended if it ultimately facilitates a sexual relationship between the couple.

Some sex therapy training courses specifically address the cultural differences of particular groups, and some sex therapists specialise in work with a particular community. For instance, orthodox Jewish couples don't have sex, or even share a bed, during menstruation or for seven days afterwards, meaning they resume sex at the most fertile point in the month. Their enforced abstinence is thought to offer an opportunity to develop non-sexual aspects of their relationship as well as increasing desire. This is important as it's seen as the man's duty to satisfy his wife. Though this is a sex-positive approach, it could increase sexual anxiety, so the work needs a therapist who understands the rationale and benefits of the religious teachings.

Some religions take virginity very seriously, to the point that some women have hymen reconstruction surgery before marriage. Prohibitions on sexual behaviour, dress and mixing mean some couples have virtually no sex education or experience and unrealistic expectations about sex. However, many religions encourage sex as an important part of a loving relationship.

INTEGRATION

Cultural needs can be taken into account and incorporated into sex therapy, though issues are most likely to arise with the core CBT approach. Many of the other ways of working could still be continued when the couple are unable to engage in sensate focus, for instance. Work on general aspects of the relationship, attitudes to sex and sexual image, management of anxiety and self-validation could all be helpfully addressed when touching isn't possible.

All the methods mentioned in this chapter can be used alone but are often incorporated with the CBT approach.

CHAPTER SUMMARY

- The original approach to sex therapy developed by Masters and Johnson, using CBT and incorporating sensate focus, can be augmented with other approaches.
- These can also be used alone.

FURTHER READING

Anderson, F., Sweezy, M. & Schwartz, R. (2017) *Internal Family Systems Skills Training Manual*, Eau Claire, WI: Pesi Publishing.

Campbell, C. (2020) *Contemporary Sex Therapy*, Abingdon, UK: Routledge.

Friday, N. (2001) *My Secret Garden*, London: Quartet Books.

Nagoski, E. (2021) *Come As You Are*, updated edition, London: Simon & Schuster.

Weiner, L. & Avery-Clark, C. (2017) *Sensate Focus in Sex Therapy*, New York: Routledge.

RESOURCES

The Strange Situation Experiment: www.youtube.com/watch?v=QTsew NrHUHU.

The Wheel of Consent: https://bettymartin.org.

BIBLIOGRAPHY

Bancroft, J., Graham, C.A., Janssen, E., & Sanders, S.A. (2009) The dual control model: Current status and future directions, *Journal of Sex Research*, 46(2–3), 121–142.

Crittenden, P. (2012) Personal communication.

Hertlein, K.M., Gambescia, N. & Weeks, G. (2019) *Systemic Sex Therapy*, 3rd edn, New York: Routledge.

Janssen, E. & Bancroft, J. (2006) The dual control model: the role of sexual inhibition & excitation in sexual arousal and behaviour. In Janssen, E. (ed.) *The Psychophysiology of Sex*, Bloomington, IN: Indiana University Press.

Krenshaw, K. (1988) Demarginalizing the intersection of race and sex: A black feminist critique of antidiscrimination doctrine, feminist theory and anti-racist politics, *University of Chicago Legal Forum*, 1, 139–167.

Martin, B. (2021) *The Art of Giving and Receiving*, Eugene, OR: Luminaire Press.

McKergow, M. (2021) *The Next Generation of Solution Focused Practice*, Abingdon, UK: Routledge.

SEXUALITY AND GENDER IDENTITY

Some therapists specialise in work with sexual and gender identity, but the way these are felt, experienced and expressed affect all of us. It's therefore important that everyone working with sex and relationships has some understanding of the different identities they may meet, and an ability to help clients explore their own identity and its expression.

SEXUALITY

Providing a neat definition of sexuality is incredibly difficult, as it encompasses both the way we see ourselves and our behaviour. This can be much more complex than it first appears. For instance, someone may identify as gay but actually be living in a straight relationship. Or someone may have regular gay encounters while identifying as straight. There isn't a definitive identity, because sexuality is experienced differently by each of us and this can change over a lifetime. Sexuality isn't just about what sort of sex you're having or who it's with, but also about how you feel and express what you feel. Some of us ooze sexuality while others are hardly aware of expressing sexuality at all. Sexuality may be an internal process, which may not be readily noticeable to anyone else but may be noticed constantly by the person experiencing it. They may, for instance, be just as aware of their sexuality as they wait for a bus as they are when engaged in a sexual act. It's also possible to enjoy sex and be aware of one's own sexuality without necessarily having much sexual confidence.

DOI: 10.4324/9781003265641-5

Some people need help to feel okay about exploring and knowing the sexual aspects of themselves and being aware of sexuality in everyday life. Few of us notice the messages we receive about sex and relationships or the rules we've internalised. Since these messages are largely directed towards the promotion of straight **cis** relationships, we acquire a great many ideas about how relationships should be which definitely don't suit them all. As well as expectations about the trappings of commitment – a home, children, pets, a 'steady' job – there are expectations that good sex – preferably, great sex – happens when partners can recognise and meet each other's needs. There's a lot asked of us and we may feel bad about ourselves if we think we're not doing sex and relationships in the way we should be, or everyone else is. Yet we mostly don't even realise we have a choice about accepting prevalent norms and labels, because we've grown up with them. We're used to them, so we don't often consider how or why they started. We may assume it's natural to live in families with two straight parents, for example – but why? Well, from a state's point of view, organising people into families with children means the population will look after itself. Parents will choose to work in order to support their family, rather than wander around only working when money runs out and possibly not having children who eventually join the workforce.

The idea that anything but a traditional nuclear family is morally wrong and unnatural is a social invention. Historically, people have lived in clans, tribes, *communities* which evolved over time into large multigenerational households which provided a workforce for their farms or businesses as well as offering childcare and support for the elderly. The idea of a forever marriage for love, and that one person could fulfil the other's every need, fuel a relatively recent romantic fantasy which still usually relies on women prioritising the needs of their partner and children above themselves.

The term *nuclear family* began to be used after World War II to describe two parents and their children living together. Nuclear comes from 'nucleus', meaning the core or base family unit. The *extended family* refers to the wider family, such as aunts, uncles, cousins and grandparents.

The industrial revolution disbanded supportive communities and large family units in order to mobilise the workforce. People were expected to move away from their extended families and communities to follow jobs. It has also gradually become normalised to have a long commute to work or even to work away, at least during the week. It's often then women who are left to manage the home, children and their own job. Such social changes are often framed as freedoms, but these 'trends' are not so much liberating people as supporting the economy. It's hard to see how time- and cash-poor families really benefit, particularly when they have to buy in assistance that would previously have been available on tap.

In other words, fashions in romance, sexual norms and family life frequently aren't natural or innate characteristics of our societies at all. We're groomed to just accept them. We like seeing people in love. Romance is promoted everywhere in the media, with unhealthy interest in celebrities' relationships, and many of us overstepping in encouraging our friends and family to move in together, tie the knot or start a family. Meanwhile, making people feel different, and framing their natural instincts as an illness, is a powerful disincentive to be yourself if yourself doesn't fit. But if there are seen to be wider financial benefits from difference, social mores change to allow them. For instance, gay marriage brings stability, mortgages and insurance plans. Gay parents contribute to the economy in major ways which make their visibility profitable. They buy childcare, food, clothing, bigger homes, larger cars and tutoring – working hard and paying taxes in stable jobs to support their children who will eventually grow up and repeat the process.

Contrast this with Japan, where public displays of affection aren't encouraged, but two-parent straight cis families are normalised and diverse relationships remain mostly private. Sex is nonetheless everywhere. As well as having a thriving porn industry, which includes films, cartoons and video games, the country has a very open interest in kink which can even be found on television game shows. There are many sex clubs, shows and cafés, and casual sex and non-monogamy are almost universally acceptable. But relational sex appears to have become less common. A Japan Family Planning Association Survey found that nearly half of young women and a quarter of young men said they weren't interested in partnered sex at all, claiming it was too much trouble. Meanwhile, Japan has one of the world's lowest birth rates. Japan's government has consequently been trying to boost straight marriage and motherhood. Though many young people do still like the idea of romance, the realities of marriage and children don't appeal. Without social or religious pressure to conform, many people never even date, let alone have sex, though there is little research into the prevalence of GSRD marginalised relationships, apart from asexuality. Perhaps they are the ones that continue to thrive.

When we appreciate how societies are engineered to promote values which are expedient rather than innate, it's clear we need to be aware of historical and social influences on the way relationships and sex are organised in order to help clients choose what works for them rather than settling for what they think ought to work.

IDENTIFYING AS STRAIGHT

Most **cisgender** straight people think very little about their sexuality and how it's expressed, because it's often assumed someone is straight unless they tell you otherwise. Non-straight and non-cis people are more likely to give considerable thought to the way they identify and to how and whether they will share this information with others. So some straight cis people can be relatively unaware of their sexual selves, and may need more help to notice what makes them feel like a sexual being or even their sexual triggers. A useful exercise can be to ask straight clients to consider what they would include in a document testifying, or coming out, as straight. They may realise their sexuality is more complex than they assumed. Often people feel there are multiple conditions to be fulfilled before they can behave sexually. These may include elements such as attraction, comfort, opportunity, context, type of relationship and sexual preferences. These usually aren't specific to just one kind of sexual identity.

If you think about it, affixing labels such as 'gay' or 'straight' has created a problem where none actually needs to exist. Applying a social constructionist or feminist lens to sexuality, it's clear these labels have invented categories which are not necessarily helpful. Suggesting one way of being is 'normal', and the other ways are different, inevitably creates shame and suggests coercion is 'acceptable'.

Social Constructionism is a way of thinking about the world that doesn't take anything for granted. Rather than just accepting that there's a right, wrong, natural or normal way to go about our lives, it explores where behaviours and ideas come from, noting how they change over time. Not so long ago, for instance, sex outside marriage was considered scandalous (even though it happened a lot); now it's considered more unusual if someone marries without ever having sexual experiences. Social constructionism also accepts that the same experience, behaviour or situation may appear very different to people or be affected by the context in which these occur.

There's a prevalent belief that sex should be much better than okay, and that partners should be servicing each other's needs. Indeed, sex is presented as something that has to be learned, perfected and performed regularly yet spontaneously and enthusiastically. If this doesn't happen, we're primed to believe there must be something wrong. Of course, this is rubbish, but the majority of our clients arrive with very clear ideas about how sex *ought* to be and how they're failing.

As therapists, it's important we don't fall into the trap of assuming we must collude with unhelpful **discourses** which are impossible to fulfil, just because this is what someone has brought to therapy. By all means respect their point of view, but do also explore more realistic ideas and discover what could be good enough sex (see also page 91). Another trap is to *assume* that apparently straight couples do identify this way or that they wish to follow a traditional trajectory. At least one partner in many couples may identify as transgender, bi or pansexual, enjoy kink, be comfortably polyamorous or into hook-ups rather than, or as well as, long relationships.

Hook-ups and occasional sex which *turn into* longer, more serious relationships bring their own issues. The way someone wants to be known in a casual encounter may be very different from the persona they wish to convey when the relationship becomes more intimate. Up until then, they may have engaged in or refused sexual experiences because the relationship was assumed to be temporary, or even faked pleasure and now want to rewind. This can bring them into therapy where this is revealed to the therapist in history taking.

It's important for therapists to be more exploratory and curious when working with people and relationships that appear knowable and familiar as well as those which are outside their personal experience. Otherwise, we can miss or close down much useful information and therapeutic opportunity.

STRAIGHT MEN WHO HAVE SEX WITH MEN (MSM)

This is not the same as experimental sex with boys at school or about being curious or bisexual. Some men frequently have sex with other men, with no interest in a relationship, and insist they identify as straight. Research with MSM suggests that they do so because their primary sexual and only *romantic* interest is in women, and they aren't involved with a gay community. Research into MSM tends to focus on problems rather than acknowledging that the men themselves don't see it this way.

Some studies say straight men have sex with men because their partners don't want sex as often as they do, and they find this an easy way to get it, often through hook-up apps. Another reason is that most don't see sex with another man as infidelity, though partners may not agree if they find out. For some, studies suggest, it's about opportunity and domination, a way of showing other men who's boss. Several researchers have noted men who identify as heteroflexible, sometimes engaging in sex together whilst watching hetero-porn. A hallmark is often a wish to persuade straight friends into sex with them, and a dislike of camp men. Indeed, the behaviour has been noted to improve some men's masculine identity, especially when it involves sex with 'butch' black men. Some younger straight men become sex workers with men when they realise this is a source of income, but never have sex with men for their own pleasure and continue to have relationships with women.

Having sex with men may be mentioned by clients in history taking and should be taken at face value. If the client identifies as straight, be clear in your own mind about why *you* want to categorise them differently. Despite the issues mentioned above, for most MSM this isn't something they need to explore in therapy. It may, however, be appropriate to check they're prioritising safer sex, especially if they have a partner, and especially if the partner is expressing dissatisfaction with sex in the relationship. While it's not the therapist's place to inform them, it may be helpful to explore with the man whether he thinks having sex with men may be impacting the sexual relationship or whether he thinks his partner could find out. If she did, what does he think would happen? Great care needs to be taken not to appear pathologising, and careful consideration is also needed as to whether such a conversation is going to be helpful or just appear critical.

It's notable that there has been hardly any research about straight women who have sex with women. It's often assumed that women are more sexually fluid than men because they're 'more emotional' and, thus, more open to connection. There's been some research into young women who identify as straight and have sex with friends, but many of the women we see in sex therapy have been surprised by their strong physical attraction to another woman which has them questioning their sexuality. Equally, there are women who occasionally have sex with women, identify as straight and don't see this as having any particular significance.

We need to be aware of research, but also to be cautious. Research is often looking for problems so that solutions can be found, rather than celebrating people's pleasure in their experiences.

HOMOSEXUAL OCD

Sexologist Joe Kort says that some men with what he calls Homosexual Obsessive Compulsive Disorder (HOCD) are preoccupied with the idea they could be gay or that other people may think they are. They constantly check themselves to ensure their speech and gestures don't come across as gay and worry about the way other people look at them or comments they've made. Some may have sex with other men to test whether they're attracted to them following this experience. They may not enjoy the sex but keep repeating it in case the previous experiences were a fluke.

The obsession may have been prompted by sexual abuse, advances made by men or comments made about them. Clients can generally remember being taunted for appearing gay, advised not to seem gay, or they've heard disparaging or scary stories about relatives or family friends who were gay. Though memories are sometimes related to random playground chatter or bullying, in many cases it's close family who have instilled the fears. HOCD can be a lifelong concern or appear suddenly and unexpectedly, Kort says.

SOCIAL CHALLENGES

Theories of homosexuality didn't exist until an Austro-Hungarian psychologist coined the term in the late nineteenth century. Before this, sexual relationships were formed more on the basis of status than identity, with receptive sex having lower status than penetration. Prohibitions against non-procreative sex by religious or state organisations were aimed at creating social stability through families. As a result, practices like anal sex (sodomy) were criminalised in the UK through the Buggery Act of 1533, and not decriminalised until 1967. The law has also been used to prevent same-sex relationships from being institutionally recognised through marriage. Most shockingly, it was not until 1981 that the WHO removed homosexuality from its list of mental illnesses, and the American Psychiatric Association's DSM retained homosexuality as a psychiatric diagnosis until 1973.

Though much of the world continues to stigmatise, and even criminalise, gay and non-binary identities, here in the UK they're much more visible. It's consequently easy to assume if you're straight that there's no longer any stigma associated with them. The reality for many people is very different. HOCD wouldn't exist if people weren't still receiving messages that only straight identity is okay, even though this is improving.

Though it's important to explore the experience and impact on *all* clients, those who are older will have lived through fairly recent times when discrimination was absolutely the norm. There was a tough period in the 1980s, for instance, when gay sexuality was framed as incredibly problematic, both in the media and by government. There was already considerable homophobia, which became worse when HIV/AIDS came along, as it was seen at the time as primarily a condition affecting gay men. This wasn't helped by the then Conservative government's emphasis on the benefits of the traditional nuclear family. It led to a draconian over-reaction when *The Daily Mail* ran a campaign suggesting that left-wing councils were damaging family values through the contents of their libraries. Chief among the accused books was one called *Jenny Lives with Eric and Martin* by Susanne Bösche, about a girl being brought up by gay dads. This book is credited with prompting legislation banning the promotion of homosexuality or of suggesting that homosexual families were acceptable. This edict was contained in Section 28, or Clause 28, of the Local Government Act 1988 which also amended the Local Government Act 1986, affecting England, Wales and Scotland.

SECTION 28

Implementation of Section 28 didn't just mean the removal of books from libraries. Many supportive youth groups and services closed, and schools were prevented from offering information or advice which could be seen as promoting homosexuality. *All* young people were disadvantaged by Section 28 as it meant sex education returned to being little more than biological information about reproduction and periods. For young people exploring their sexual or gender identity, there was absolutely nowhere to turn for guidance. Many felt obliged to adopt a secretive approach to their identity and adapt their behaviour to fit in with the prevailing discourses around sexuality.

Section 28 was not repealed until 2000 in Scotland and 2003 in England and Wales, by which time many young people had missed out on much needed information and advice. This included straight people who developed stereotypical ideas about gender and sex. Failure to explore ideas about what sex means and is has, for instance, encouraged unhelpful beliefs about sex as performative, with the emphasis on intercourse and orgasm rather than exploration and intimacy. It also promoted the adoption of **heteronormative** ideas about gay sex and relationships, such as that all gay men enjoy anal penetration or that all lesbian women hate intercourse.

It's now feared we are in danger of returning to the negative and uninformed thinking which led to Section 28. Stonewall, for instance, which was established in 1988 to oppose Section 28, has made comparisons with recent government backtracking on trans rights. This includes reneging on a pledge to allow trans people to self-identify as the gender they choose on their birth certificates and restricting access to healthcare for transgender children and young people (see also page 132).

IDENTIFYING AS A GAY MAN

As always, it's important not to assume that an individual or couple's issues are necessarily related to being gay. It's nonetheless important to ask generally whether they've had struggles in their lives. How someone or a couple has managed difficulties can be used to boost resilience and find solutions going forward. Many clients will have felt marginalised or oppressed at some stage, whether due to their sexual identity or something else, and we still often meet **internalised homophobia**. Some clients, especially older ones, seek explanations for their sexuality or believe there's something wrong with them that could potentially be fixed. We need to be clear that, while we're happy to help someone explore their sexuality, we *never* offer therapy to change someone's sexual orientation. Clients who want to do so are often from countries where sexuality is controlled, from families with heteronormative expectations or are older and have been living in straight relationships. They may have witnessed the homophobia of family and colleagues and be worried that they will be ostracised if they come out. Fewer than half of people who are marginalised in relation to their GSRD identities feel comfortable being open about this with all their family members, Stonewall research has found. It also noted significant discrimination or bullying in education, healthcare, at work and in sport.

On the other hand, it should never be *assumed* that someone has necessarily had a difficult time. Someone's sexuality shouldn't be the focus of therapy unless they want it to be, so stereotypical ideas about gay sexuality aren't helpful. Many gay men are comfortable just being themselves and don't feel required either to conform or to reject identities, so once again don't presume. There's a careful line to walk between being intrusive or stereotyping and not being interested enough in someone's experience. A particular danger may be feeling strongly identified with a client who is superficially similar, but whose experience is actually very different to the therapist's. This can lead to incorrect assumptions about the client and unconscious attempts to make them fit.

Though there's no one-size-fits-all definition of a gay man, there is evidence that many gay men worry about being 'good enough' or fitting in. As a result, it's thought some subcultures have developed whose members feel more comfortable relating to the group identity. There are also subcultures within subcultures, suggesting a strong need to experience a close and supportive fit. If they want to, it can be helpful to explore how someone's labelled or preferred identity differs from their actual performance of the identity.

> Men who engage in anal sex may self-identify as *tops* who prefer an insertive role, *bottoms* who choose a receptive role or *versatile* if they're flexible about this. This role may apply to all partners or change depending on who someone is with.

Often, therapy can provide joyful opportunities for gay men to explore the boundaries of their relationship or ways to expand their intimacy. Therapy can be helpful at pivotal times in a relationship, such as deciding whether to get married or start a family. As well as discussing the practicalities and options available, couples may wish to look at ways of approaching their lives together that work best for them rather than replicating **heteronormative** scripts.

TWINKS

Though therapists should not refer to them in this way, young, slim, hairless, effeminate and self-caring gay men may identify as twinks. Research suggests they manage discrimination better than some other gay subcultures, possibly because they are out and able to empathically discuss their sexuality. Many also have supportive female friends. Health professionals may be more aware of twinks' sexuality and thus more likely to mention issues like HIV status, which contrasts with other gay groups who appear more traditionally masculine.

Those identifying as twinks may experience mental health issues as they age, gain weight or acquire unwanted body hair, which can lead to low self-esteem and relationship issues. There's always a possibility that emphasis on slimness can lead to eating disorders.

BEARS

There are some highly masculine gay subcultures, which are often very organised, with their own societies and publications. These include **leathermen**, *bulls* and *bears* which have a particularly large number of subgroups.

Not to be confused with chubs, who are simply gay and heavy, bears are mostly white, hairier, heavier, shorter and more traditionally masculine than some gay men. They are, for instance, less interested in bodily aesthetics than in sexual experiences. It's been argued that they have turned their appearance to their advantage by creating a 'type' to aspire to. For instance, hairless bears are known as *manatees* and thinner bears are known as *otters*. Thinner, hairless men who are attracted to them are known as *chasers*.

As well as appearing more masculine themselves, bears may be disparaging of feminine gay men, prefer more dominant sex and engage in more risky behaviour with more partners. Indeed, health professionals are urged to be aware of gay masculine subcultures because their members may be less likely to use condoms or have HIV screening. Their high body mass index also puts them at risk of conditions such as cardiovascular disease and diabetes, but they may be resistant to health messages as their size is so important to their identity. It's therefore essential that health professionals approach size issues with sensitivity and interest in the individual's motivation and beliefs. Sex therapists may be more able to accept that clients are comfortable with their weight than other health workers with a particular agenda, and so better able to empathise with its role in identity formation.

Twinks and bears have been mentioned here to demonstrate the contrast in identity presentation among gay men. It nonetheless remains important to be curious about individuals' identity and not to assume a label, keeping in mind that there are scores of gay subcultures. One reason that it may be so important to feel a sense of belonging is that gay men have experienced so much judgement, both from within and outside their communities. For instance, many gay men report experiencing pressure to come out or to engage in sexual practices they don't feel ready for or just don't appeal, alongside pressure to hide their sexuality or not to be gay at all.

As the bear community was emerging in the 1980s, so were groups of men who used drugs and partying to manage their distress. Public reactions to the then new risks from HIV/AIDS increased homophobia, particularly as there were popular discourses around the idea that HIV was a punishment for sexual deviance. Individuals who were coming to terms with their sexuality and feeling accepted were suddenly feeling threatened from within and by others. Not knowing whether they had acquired an infection, they were nonetheless assumed to be infectious by frightened members of the public responding to headlines about a 'gay plague'.

Sexual wellbeing advocate and activist David Stuart was among the gay men who took part in drug binges which could last for several days. Crystal meth, mephedrone and GHB are the main drugs used, creating extreme highs and a sense of intimacy. Stuart coined the term chemsex in the 1990s, realising that health care was needed but trying to demonstrate that what he and other men were experiencing was much more complex than just drug addiction. The men were seeking connection in place of isolation and release from chronic feelings of trauma and shame. Chemsex provided a sense of identity and belonging. For many men, chemsex still meets these needs, and they're able to use it without developing any problems or dependency. For others, it can create more problems than it solves.

Sex therapists may see clients who've been through a period of chemsex involvement in the past, which may or may not have been problematic, or who may be attempting to change now. Sometimes physical or mental health issues prompt this, as the disinhibition associated with the drugs can, for instance, result in physical injury caused by rough sex, sexually transmitted infections and mental health issues related to chronic use. Some people also feel even more isolated, as their social life becomes dictated by hook-up apps and parties where they move from one lover to another. Many have not had a real friendship, partner or sober sex for many years.

Therapy is more likely to be helpful if the individual feels understood and heard rather than judged and launched immediately into an addiction programme. Gradually helping them to regain a sense of self-worth and efficacy, plus treatment of their trauma and low self-esteem, may help these clients find different ways of managing. Specialist sexual health clinics can provide practical assistance with STI treatment (see also pages 146–150), strategies to assist with quitting chemsex and appropriate emotional support.

IDENTIFYING AS A GAY WOMAN

Research suggests that women who have sex with women are more sexually satisfied than women in straight relationships. Having a lover who understands their bodies and their experiences is thought to be the reason. Just like gay men, though, lesbian women have been subject to categorisation. Particular descriptors are *butch* and *femme* or *lipstick lesbians*, potentially a hangover from heteronormative ways of considering them. A straight assumption that lesbian couples inevitably split into male and female roles is not supported by reality. Though some couples may replay relationship scripts they identify with, this is not an innate feature of same-sex couples. Regrettably, there remain therapists and health professionals who cause deep offence by assuming this. As ever, it's important to find out about the individuals and how *they* identify.

Some women have had relationships with men by the time they come out and, like men, may present for therapy when they're leaving a long straight relationship. For some this is a relief, while others struggle with **internalised homophobia**, guilt about the effect on children, their ex or other family members. Some want to look at their lifelong sexuality, wondering whether they've always really been gay or whether they just responded to another woman who understands their mind and body so much better than their male partner. Younger couples may have explored their sexuality while still in school, and may be more secure in their sexuality, but nothing should be assumed.

Many lesbian couples enjoy penetrative vaginal or anal sex using **strap-ons**, sex toys and fingers, but many don't – so always check if this is appropriate to their therapy. Just like anyone, lesbian couples can have enjoyable sex lives or struggle with them in some way. Specific to their sexuality is the myth of *Lesbian Bed Death*. This assumes that lesbian couples will cease to initiate sex after a while, as there is no testosterone-fuelled lover to maintain the sexual momentum. Another way of looking at this is just that male sexual behaviour is being applied to women. Masters and Johnson attempted to present an egalitarian frame for all sexualities, which was enthusiastically adopted but doesn't acknowledge that there *are* differences in women's sexuality. For instance, women's arousal doesn't build in a neat wave, but may ebb and flow during a sexual encounter. While sex does decline in some lesbian relationships – and this may be a 'normal' feature of them – the same can be said for most long relationships. Loss of desire is often more about familiarity, lack of opportunity and busy lives. Again, stereotypes about the couple aren't helpful.

While many same sex couples have children from previous relationships, some struggle to have their own. They may enter a private sperm donation arrangement with a man, often one who wants a child too or, like many gay men, opt for surrogacy. Lesbian women may not qualify for NHS fertility treatment if they haven't yet had difficulty becoming pregnant. They usually need to have several failed cycles of privately funded insemination before they can obtain NHS support. It's no longer possible to buy sperm for private insemination, as it has to be delivered to fertility clinics which charge for the service. This has led some couples to enter private arrangements which have fewer health checks and may even be dangerous.

IDENTIFYING AS BISEXUAL

Much of the time, someone's bisexual identity isn't relevant to the problems they're bringing to therapy. Indeed, it often won't come up at all unless it's specifically asked about. Bisexuality can be an invisible identity, as people's sexuality is understandably assumed on the basis of their partner. However, if you ask straight or gay couples about their sexuality, one or both may say they identify as bisexual or something else. For many couples, this is not an issue in the relationship, as they're into the person they're with and don't feel unsatisfied. Sometimes, their partner might worry that they are, however, and it's this anxiety which can create problems. In such cases, exploring how the anxiety is managed can highlight examples of resilience in the relationship which can be utilised in the therapy.

Studies suggest that bisexuality is associated with more mental health issues, suicidality and self-harm than gay identities. However, research may be skewed towards people presenting with problems rather than the much higher numbers of people identifying as bisexual than are recognised. Where mental health issues do exist this may be because there is pressure to settle on a gay or straight identity, or individuals are presumed to be on the way to settling, as if bisexuality is a phase. There is also some hostility toward the term bisexual, as it has been accused of being *trans-exclusionary*. Though terms like *pansexuality* and *sexual fluidity* may appear to have a more all-encompassing tone, the term bisexuality is not trans-exclusionary as it simply refers to attraction to people who are the same *and* different.

ASEXUALITY

Asexuality, or ace, is a spectrum of sexual interest, or lack of it. It's frequently confused with celibacy and/or being a loner, but many people identifying as asexual do have sex and/or relationships. Some people experience sexual attraction too, but only in certain circumstances or contexts, or may have personal rules about who, when, how or why they act on it. So asexuality shouldn't be seen as a blanket description. It's far more complex than that. Some people who identify as on the asexual spectrum have no interest in sex or romance and don't masturbate. Others may not be interested in partnered sex, or may be interested in partnered sex but not in relationships. Some may have no strong feelings about sex, so will engage in sexual behaviours if their partner wants to, but wouldn't go out of their way to do so.

GREY-A

This refers to people who very rarely experience sexual attraction or engage in sexual behaviour. For instance, someone who has never experienced sexual attraction may find that they one day do, and then assume the Grey-A identity even if they never experience sexual attraction again.

DEMI-SEXUALITY

Sexual attraction which develops once you get to know someone is known as demi-sexuality. It used to be far less problematic than it has become now that having sex before or without a relationship is normalised for many people.

A-ROMANTICS

A-Romantics don't feel a romantic attraction to other people, though that doesn't mean they won't bond with someone. They may or may not engage in sexual behaviour. If they do bond it'll be in the form of a partnership rather than a romance, sometimes known as *Queerplatonic*.

SPLIT ATTRACTION

The Split Attraction Model distinguishes between romantic and sexual attraction, meaning that someone could be romantically attracted to anybody but only sexually attracted to other genders. The asexualities all have a romantic counterpart; for example, *Grey-Romantic* and *Demi-Romantic*.

THERAPY WITH ASEXUAL CLIENTS

Sex therapists quickly become aware that many people aren't particularly, or at all, interested in sex. Some couples present because the asexual partner would like to feel more interest in order to please the other. Or they present alone, believing there's something wrong with them. It may have been hard for them to find advice, as asexuality is often misunderstood. Well-meaning health professionals, youth workers and parents may advise someone they'll grow out of it, so they inevitably feel there's something wrong with them when they don't.

Sometimes, people who are not attracted to a partner – frequently in an abusive relationship – are told by a health professional that asexuality explains their lack of interest. This kind of mistake makes it essential not to apply labels ourselves. We can offer information and see how it lands, but we need to be curious and seek explanations which are a good fit for the client rather than an easy option for ourselves.

There's a difference between losing interest in sex at a time when life is especially stressful or tiring and never being interested. Though this may change, many people identifying as asexual feel their absence of sexual interest has been lifelong. Some discover asexuality after years in a relationship and realise that it describes them. Often, their partners worry that they no longer find them sexually attractive, not realising that they never did. They may have had the relationship simply because they felt expected to have a partner or they may genuinely love them and be attracted to other qualities than their sexual appeal. Even when they find sex is bonding or physically gratifying, many people could cheerfully live without it. For them, sex may have never involved desire. Even if they enjoy sex when it happens, they may be entirely comfortable with the idea that it could never happen again.

There's so much pressure to be sexual that many people experience considerable shame when they don't feel sexual interest or attraction. Indeed, although some may find that asexuality describes their experience, they resist the description because it seems so stigmatising. Others find the concept of asexuality extremely helpful in explaining how they feel.

Partnered sex may have never been of interest for some people, but they've gone along with it out of obligation and expectation, eventually realising they don't have to. Needless to say, this can be difficult for partners, but some see sex as their right and expect therapy to support this. This is not the therapist's role. It's important to be sensitive to individual experience and wishes, and to adequately explore what the asexual partner really wants. They may genuinely wish to be able to be sexual with someone they deeply love, and sex therapy may be able to establish what's possible. Nonetheless, there's a danger of colluding with non-consensual sexual experiences if one partner is agreeing to therapy only to please the other. While it may be hugely painful to be in a relationship with someone you love and/or find sexually attractive who doesn't feel the same way, sex with someone who doesn't want it can never be okay. While it's true that most people have occasionally gone along with sex when they were tired or not in the mood, this is very different from sex that always feels wrong and is allowed rather than freely given. While some couples may want to experiment with what's possible, there should never be an assumption that asexuality is something to fix or just a matter of different sex drives.

SEXUAL AVERSION DISORDER

This condition is worth mentioning, as it crops up in DSM-5 under the category of 'other specified sexual dysfunctions'. As it's unlikely that someone would present with this unless encouraged by their partner, and as there's likely to be a reason for their aversion, treatment of their disgust may be considered unethical. It could be that the client is comfortably asexual, but it's more likely that relationship issues are causing the aversion or that there's a trauma history which needs to be addressed. Approaches like couple counselling or EMDR can be offered for relationship distress and trauma, but care needs to be taken not to suggest this will be treatment for any form of sexual identification or preference. If someone has decided they don't like or want sex, that's their business and not our job to try to change even when – or especially when – a partner feels entitled to sex.

MONOGAMY

Problems with monogamy are not necessarily about affairs, but about expectations. Managing monogamy often brings couples into therapy, as each partner may have different assumptions about what it means. Most couples don't realise that they need to manage their monogamy or even think about it. However, it's unlikely that two people will have exactly the same ideas about how relationships should be, and it's this difference that often emerges in couples' arguments. Commonly, each assumes the other understands and shares their values but is deliberately flouting them. What's more, social and cultural changes make a difference to what's acceptable.

Most people nowadays have periods of non-monogamy where once they would have practised serial monogamy, with periods of celibacy between 'steady' partners. Many people regularly have casual or hook-up sex with someone without identifying as a couple. Whether or not they think commitment should be overtly discussed or is implicit may be different for each partner. Then, within a 'committed' relationship, even when monogamy is assumed to be a feature of their commitment, this may mean different things to each of them. Does 'forsaking all other' mean never 'liking' an ex's post on social media, for instance? The monogamy quiz may be helpful for both therapists and their clients to recognise their assumptions and what they may need to negotiate. Tick answers you find appropriate and consider why this is, using the end notes to help and discussing with your partner(s) how your answers differ.

MONOGAMY QUIZ

Which of the following behaviours would you say are acceptable in a monogamous relationship?

A – Finding other people attractive
A – Fantasising about someone else during sex
A – Occasionally watching pornography alone

B – Following an ex-partner on social media
B – Continuing friendly, non-sexual contact with an ex
B – Staying in touch with an ex's family

C – Blowing kisses
C – Non-sexual kisses or hugs with other people
C – Holding hands with friends

D – Multiple friendly texts to a work colleague every day
D – Going for a drink after work with someone you know is interested in you

D – Confiding in someone else about your relationship
E – Having sex because you feel obliged to
E – Refusing sex to punish your partner
E – No social behaviour other than with your partner or with their knowledge and permission
E – Shelving a sexual interest if your partner doesn't like it

G – Swinging
G – Visiting fetish clubs together
G – Telling each other about past relationships

H – Sexting

H – Cybersex

H – Watching strippers, flirting or sexual touch during a hen or stag night

H – Sex with someone else that stops short of penetration

H – Occasional hook-ups

H – Use of sex workers

H – Affairs that the partner is unaware of

H – Sex with someone else if a partner does not want sex

As – These are all personal behaviours which don't affect your partner, so some couples would be okay with these. But some find it hard not to know what's going on in each other's heads. This is fine if they both feel the same way, but can feel a bit stifling if not.

Bs – This is an area where couples may differ. There are no right or wrong answers and a great deal may depend on the individual situation, but some people have strong feelings about contact with an ex in any circumstances.

Cs – How you feel about this may depend on the kind of family you come from and whether they went in for much physical affection. It's sometimes necessary to learn to manage your own feelings if you find this uncomfortable in a partner.

Ds – Some of us will think that any or all of these are fine, that it depends on the context or that they're never okay.

Es – Probably everyone has had sex at some point to please their partner, but they should feel they have a choice. Sex becomes weaponised in many relationships that the couple consider loving. Sex and intimacy are not just about penetration and orgasm. Negotiating how to behave when this isn't wanted can allow warm cuddles or a little fooling around rather than no contact at all.

Gs – All of these need active and ongoing agreement from both partners.

Hs – These are sexual behaviours which could be considered non-monogamies if the partner doesn't know about them.

With all these categories, communication is crucial along with an awareness that feelings can change.

How often have you done the following?

A – Discussed what monogamy means to you with your partner

A – Revisited that definition

A – Negotiated boundaries explicitly

A – Regularly checked in as to how this is going

B – Worried that your behaviour may have crossed a line

C – Defended your behaviour to a partner who thinks you've crossed a line

C – Asked someone other than your partner whether they think your behaviour is okay

A – The more As you've ticked, the better you probably understand each other and respect each other's viewpoints. You realise the importance of putting effort into your relationship. If you have few As, you probably need to make time to negotiate the nature of your relationship.

B – You're human.

C – Though some partners are controlling and jealous, this is often used as a justification for behaviour someone knows would not be acceptable to their partner.

It's important we remain curious about our clients' relationships and don't impose our own assumptions or buy into theirs. Frequently, straight couples in particular haven't negotiated the boundaries of their relationship at all and are surprised to discover they don't agree. If creating boundaries sounds restrictive, this can be reimagined as the agreements which make the relationship special. Couples often just take monogamy to mean not having sex with anyone else. But what constitutes sex? For one partner this may only mean **PiV** intercourse, while for others flirting or text messaging would be seen as a serious indiscretion. Some people think same-sex liaisons, non-penetrative experiences or secrecy makes a relationship monogamous. If these have been agreed upon, both partners may see it that way but there's a risk of real shock or pain if they both don't agree or don't know – unless not knowing is the agreement.

Identifying what makes their relationship special can help to futureproof it, as couples learn to be more appreciative and value what they have. On the other hand, some couples may only have sex with each other but not really enjoy each other's company, and get far more pleasure from their relationships with friends, colleagues and family members. If their fidelity is all that's keeping the relationship going – and it frequently *is* what couples say proves they're in love – they may choose to rethink their connection and how it could be improved. Far too often, couples seek support, thinking their sex life or whole relationship is broken when they simply aren't aware of their different viewpoints and certainly haven't discussed them.

POLYAMORY

Consensual non-monogamy takes many forms, of which polyamory is one. It isn't about **swinging**, having an affair or turning a blind eye. Polyamory refers to openness to having sexual, loving or romantic relationships with more than one person. It's implied that all involved partners are aware of all the relationships involved. The definitions have broadened considerably in recent times, as people discover many ways of interpreting polyamory that work for them. Sometimes polyamory is hierarchical, with a single primary partner and then secondary or tertiary partners, with the main partner known as the *vee*. Additional casual relationships are known as *orbits*. Though the partners of partners may or may not be personally known to other members of the formation, the entire group has been known as a *polycule*.

Sometimes there is more equality in partners' status. This doesn't necessarily mean they live together, but they have equivalent importance in their poly partner's life. This may have evolved because more people are being open about their polyamory. In the past, there's been considerable judgement about it, so having a 'stable' couple at the heart of a poly constellation may have been perceived as more acceptable. Indeed, many poly people report judgement from therapists who presume polyamory is causing their problems. However, if their polyamory isn't the reason for the therapy, it may not be appropriate to concentrate on it, and certainly not to look for issues.

It's important for therapists to be aware of their own responses and how they're managing them. If you find the whole concept of polyamory challenging, maybe you're not a good fit for therapy with a poly couple. However, consider that these days many people actually start out as polyamorous, having a number of sexual and/or romantic relationships with little or no commitment. That's not to say that poly relationships aren't committed.

However, it's unrealistic to expect that a single relationship could possibly fulfil all one's needs, and some people manage this through polyamory. Multiple concurrent relationships aren't new either, as in the past they've been much more accepted. The idea of a couple who fulfil each other's needs is relatively recent.

Poly couples often present with problems when one partner wants some sort of change. This can happen if there's a difference in their circumstances involving a big commitment, such as starting a family or going to live abroad, rather than with the nature of the relationship itself. It can, nonetheless, be useful to explore whether a poly couple have created adequate boundaries and agreements about the way their relationships will work and to enquire how they're managing any jealousy. Whether they're out about the nature of the relationship may be relevant, as sometimes issues arise from the attitude of family and friends.

Some people are part of a polyamorous community whose members support each other's lifestyle. The sense of belonging can be helpful for people who feel marginalised, especially if other friends and family are judgemental or unsupportive. In therapy, though, we may see couples in the early stages of **opening up** who are looking for help in negotiating the boundaries of a new way of relating. Sometimes one partner is driving this and the other may be going along with it for fear the relationship will otherwise end. Indeed, introducing polyamory *is* sometimes a way of ending a relationship gradually, possibly in the hope it will be the other partner who actually makes the decision to split. Once again, though, this shouldn't be assumed. Other relationships can offer a break and freshness which invigorates a primary relation-ship, particularly when a partner is still in love but finding this a bit stifling.

Calling what they're doing polyamory can sometimes be used as a way of managing serial affairs, when both partners feel it removes shame from their situation. This is rarely true polyamory, but more likely to be a case of someone putting up with a situation they can't change. This may satisfy both partners, however, and not be the reason they're seeking help. Consequently, they may quit therapy if they feel judged.

Of course, it can also be hard for the original partner to accept the idea that someone else is now as important as they are, even if a poly relationship was their idea in the first place. There's an expectation that poly partners will aim for **compersion**, and find joy in the other's pleasure about the new relationship, but this can be easier said than done. Many poly partners claim to feel it, and there's no doubt many of them do, but it's also human to experience jealousy and to miss a partner when they're not around. It can be especially difficult to witness someone in the throes of new relationship energy (NRE) when they are very focused on the novel qualities of their new love.

SERIAL NRE

Some people feel they need the thrill of new relationships and hop from one to another in serial fashion. Sometimes they may neglect, and even resent, their primary or other partner(s) so that other relationships run into difficulties. They may add another partner as the NRE wears off or just end relationships when they cease to be as exciting.

Cultural expectations around having a single long-term relationship are not exclusive to straight, cis relationships. Poly communities can also prefer hierarchical relationships with a central couple and see serial relationships as problematic. People who have them sometimes appear in therapy when partners or their poly community have rejected them, either angry with what they see as misunderstanding or wanting to explore why they need to keep moving. They may need help with self-regulation if they've been using NRE to manage their emotions. They may also benefit from more systemic exploration of their expectations around relationships and the reality that NRE wears off and is replaced by a more enduring connection which requires effort to sustain. However, some people wouldn't be able to sustain a longer relationship without short ones as well, or may feel more able to be themselves in short relationships. There are multiple reasons why this may work for someone, so the emphasis may need to be more on how this is managed than changing it, depending on what the individual wants.

RELATIONSHIP ANARCHISTS

Relationship anarchists see all relationships as equal, not differentiating between, say, a family member, friend or someone they have a sexual or romantic connection with. Because no one relationship is prioritised, partners of relationship anarchists sometimes seek therapy to cope with their wish to be treated as more important. However, it's generally the case that they were always aware of their partner's attitudes, but either didn't really believe them or thought they could change them. While they may hope their therapist will join them in stigmatising relationship anarchy, this is not appropriate. Therapy can help them manage their disappointment, but also work on their attitude to boundaries and consent. Sometimes there's a **fantasy bond**, where the client has been projecting more romance onto the relationship than actually existed.

GENDER

We've already established that identity is not fixed and that the way we look at different identities is strongly affected by our families, culture and religion. Gender is just the same. While biological sex is assigned at birth on the basis of whether the baby's genitals appear more male or female, gender is much more personal. It has been argued that gender is a performance which is influenced by our culture and others' expectations of us. However, those who are content in their assigned gender (**cisgender**) usually don't think about this very much at all. Even though we have established routines which service the gender we perform, such as putting on makeup, shaving or choosing certain clothes, that's not necessarily something we dwell on. We may not even be aware that these behaviours confirm our gender to ourselves. But for some of us, it's a lot more complicated, and gender is something that's thought about constantly.

Those of us who don't feel the way our assigned biological sex suggests we would are said to be experiencing *gender dysphoria*. For instance, we may be assigned male sex at birth but feel female, or we may experience gender changes depending on context, the way we're treated or our mood. Though there are many people who would prefer not to be labelled at all, anyone who feels discomfort with their assigned gender may identify in a variety of ways which feel like a better fit.

Gender expansive ways of being which subvert traditional expectations include fluid, queer and androgynous identities. Some people don't want others to be able to tell what gender they are from the way they appear or their names and others may wish to present in a way that confuses taken-for-granted gender.

Third gender has traditionally referred to recognised genders in other parts of the world, such as South Asia and Africa, which include characteristics of the opposite gender that exist between the genders or have neither of the binary genders. For instance, Native Americans recognise Two Spirit people as being both genders simultaneously. It's sometimes adopted now by communities which are marginalised in relation to their GSRD identities as *another* way of being, such as pangender or queer identity.

The box containing examples of gender identities describes some of these, but there are many more. It's really important to ascertain how people identify and like to be referred to, and to respect this. For instance, it can be useful to enquire about preferred personal pronouns on booking paperwork or during an initial assessment.

GENDER IDENTITIES

Agender: Feeling genderless.

Cisgender: Gender identity is the same as the gender at birth.

Cishet: Gender identity and sexuality reflect the gender binary; that is, someone identifies with the gender assigned at birth and is attracted to the opposite sex.

Genderfluid: Gender identity and performance is variable.

Genderqueer: Identifying as no single gender.

Gender expansive/Gender non-conforming: Gender performance doesn't accord with cultural expectations.

Gendervoid: Unable to identify with a gender despite wishing they could.

Non-binary: Describes any gender identity where someone does not fully identify with the gender assigned at birth.

Omnigender: Experiencing all genders.

Pangender: Identification with elements of more than one gender.

Transgender: Gender identity differs from the gender someone was assigned at birth.

Intersex: Not actually a gender identity but an anatomical or physiological variation.

CISGENDER

People who identify as the gender they were assigned don't usually think about this until they experience some sort of challenge. Because this is often associated with changes to body shape, attraction or physical ability, it can quickly make someone avoid physical contact, leading to sex and relationship problems. Having rarely if ever previously considered the significance of their gender, they may have few resources to help them cope, and so seek therapy.

Therapists often focus on trying to reframe thoughts about the presenting problem, missing the underlying issue of gender performance. This can be complex and confusing, especially when confronted for the first time. Asked how, say, putting on weight makes a cis person feel, they'll often just come up with self-criticism, describing themselves as ugly, gross or disgusting. This may encourage their therapist to work only on replacing negative thoughts about body image. But ask someone what, say, being overweight says about them, or means to them, and they'll frequently reply that it makes them feel less of a man/woman. This may be the first time they've realised their gender expression has mattered, as it's been something they've just taken for granted.

As well as opening up conversations about the nature of attraction and intimacy, acknowledging this can help people recognise what *does* make them feel sexy or attractive and begin to explore how they learned about their gender, what they learned and how this is enacted. For some cis people, these conversations create sudden awareness that their gender was not their choice. Some can even remember moments when they realised they were stuck with their gender or of being told off for being an unladylike girl or too-emotional boy.

So, while cisgender people experience the privilege of not *having* to think about their gender, and this privilege is worth acknowledging, cis clients' relationship with their gender can be very usefully explored in therapy.

THERAPISTS' GENDER EXPRESSION

It's inevitable that we form impressions of the people we meet or, these days, see on screens in video calls. We should note our reactions and what they lead us to think or feel about the other person. We then need to call up our curiosity to use these initial impressions helpfully. So someone with a hairy face and deep voice dressed in a shirt, jeans and boots may appear to be identifying as male, but may tell you they identify as a trans woman or as gender fluid, genderqueer, gender expansive, omnigender, gender void or something else. Your own initial impression may offer information about how this person is perceived and manages this. They may be deliberately attempting to subvert conventional gender understandings, they may be exhausted by trying to perform their assigned or identified gender, they may want to be accepted for who they are. It is absolutely not therapists' role to tell people how to be or that they should pass as a 'definite' gender.

We need to consider how our clients position us when they challenge our own taken-for-granted or chosen ways of thinking. It may be that we judge clients for being too conventional-looking or too different. If this happens, we need to be able to work out what has been triggered in us.

It's also important that we consider how the way we present comes across to our clients. They too may make assumptions about *our* gender and sexuality based on the way we look. This may be something to discuss if you look very different, but present this as an option rather than insisting on it if it makes the client(s) uncomfortable. As with any form of self-disclosure, the conversation should be about the clients' process more than about the therapist. There are times when it's appropriate to self-disclose elements of our personal journeys, often in order to normalise someone else's experience, particularly a young person's. Once again, though, don't forget that superficial similarities can be very misleading, so don't assume your clients are like you just because you look alike.

EXPRESSING YOUR GENDER EXERCISE

We express, or perform, our gender in a variety of ways we may not often think about, though some aspects could reflect a deliberate attempt to be more/less masculine/feminine/non-binary etc. Use this exercise to consider how you do this and whether there's anything you would like to change.

APPEARANCE
How do your clothes, build, hair and makeup express your gender?

BODY LANGUAGE
What does your posture, physical habits and the way you move say about your gender?

VOICE
How does the way you speak and sound express gender?

BELIEFS AND ATTITUDES
Many of our beliefs and attitudes are acquired through our upbringing, culture, media and the people we mix with. Though not overtly a gender expression, they can affect both our behaviour and the way we feel about ourselves and how our gender is performed. This can instil delight, satisfaction and pride or be a source of discomfort or oppression. What is the source of messages, beliefs and attitudes which reflect your gender? Do you express any of these in spite of your gender identity?

BEHAVIOUR
Which behaviours reflect your gender identity or conflict with it? Do they reflect your beliefs or are they a reflection of someone else's views?

REFLECTIONS
What have you learned from this exercise? Does your gender expression seem complex or straightforward? Is there anything you would now like to change?

MASCULINITY

It's not just coming out with a diverse identity that makes people consider masculinity. Maleness is an extremely difficult concept to explain or, indeed, for many men to relate to. Male clients often describe their male role models, especially their fathers, in one-dimensional terms which didn't allow them to witness their dad's process in dealing with life's issues, such as fear, disappointment and loss. Men asked in therapy to describe their fathers frequently offer behaviours, such as heavy drinker, sportsman, withdrawn, absent and hard worker, rather than the more emotional descriptors used for mothers, such as kind, loving, helpful, generous, warm and funny. The emotion which *does* frequently appear for fathers is anger.

Part of this is due to *gender dichotomy*, the perception of men and women as opposites with no overlapping traits. Though we may hope few would now subscribe to this idea, in fact many elements survive and are reinforced in the way we're socialised by our families, schools, religion and the media. Some of the stereotypical understandings of masculinity include the idea that men must be tough, fearless, homophobic, competitive, beer drinking, suspicious of doctors, unemotional (apart from angry), sporty, quiche hating, financially responsible, competitive, domestically incompetent (except for DIY) and sexually insatiable. Even when these don't come naturally, some men may nonetheless feel required to perform at least some of them, often leaving them with a sense of confusion or unsettled. Meanwhile, there are men who identify with most, if not all, these traits which give them a sense of structure and may help manage or avoid feelings of shame. When there is also a sense of dominance over women, and weaker men who don't conform, this is referred to as *hegemonic masculinity*. This can be enacted in a variety of ways that may present differently; a cool playboy style is superficially unlike a driven workaholic style, for instance, though they may share characteristics, such as being financially stable and prioritising themselves.

Lack of self-examination and emotion may create health and relationship issues, but there *can* be positive attributes to this type of masculinity. Another style, for example, is an old-fashioned protective and courteous attitude towards women. This produces male dominance, but also clear roles and mutual care which may suit both partners. However, they will often seek therapy in crisis if one of their roles is disrupted by a change in circumstance or health. *Toxic masculinity* occurs where entitlement and actual disdain for women and weaker others is present, often accompanied by inability to manage emotions except by acting out or lashing out.

Clearly, not all men fit into these categories, but many men's role models may do, and there are many men struggling to work out what masculinity means to them or what's acceptable. Their wish to not be like men who overstep, assume or abuse leaves them feeling ashamed, vulnerable and ungrounded, often with little ability to understand themselves. More men like this, who are seeking therapy to explore the process of coming out as straight, may need considerable support to discover a comfortable way to relate to all others without attracting either ridicule or condemnation. Finding a sweet spot between unacceptable male attributes and those they admire may not be easy, with some men struggling to know how to express themselves or what's okay. These are often the very men who already show women respect and interest, and are quite different from those **incels** or angry men who complain of equality going too far or believe the only way to deal with women is to trick them. Men who find difficulty in expressing emotions other than anger, or who have a strong sense of entitlement in relation to women, may also need sensitive help to find their masculine comfort zone. Such men have often been shamed in childhood and may find the security of identifying with stereotypical male behaviour assuages feelings of uncertainty and humiliation.

METROSEXUALITY

The traditional view of masculinity was challenged in the 1990s by metrosexual men like footballer David Beckham who openly cared about personal grooming and clothes. Metrosexuals used cosmetics, followed fashion and removed body hair. Their sexuality was unclear but, for the first time, there were many straight men who were unfazed by sexual ambiguity. Metrosexuality has been welcomed as an example of hybrid masculinity, a deliberate borrowing of characteristics from groups which are not traditionally male, such as gay men.

Some people see this as a positive way of challenging hegemonic masculinity and disrupting male privilege. Others, however, consider it a way of perpetuating and obscuring power inequality in a world where traditional masculinity has become more problematic. Sociologists note that this appropriation of other groups' characteristics is primarily undertaken by straight white men, allowing them to pass as accepting of difference when their behaviour actively promotes inequality. An example is the way gay and ethnically vibrant areas in cities have been appropriated by the straight community, leading to soaring house prices and an influx of white professionals, thereby excluding many black and ethnic communities and people with marginalised GSRD identities.

FEMININITY

Many women and girls experience enormous pressure to conform to cultural notions of femininity which are presented to them as innate or natural, such as being softly spoken, gentle, pretty, obliging and uncomplaining. Unsurprisingly, they often discover they have strong feelings about the way they express their femininity – or choose not to. However, conscious attempts to manage femininity may relate primarily to appearance and a sense of being either objectified or admired. Clients may be much less aware of a felt requirement to perform feminine 'characteristics' such as empathy, kindness and common sense, being used to just performing these. Some may protest, though, that they have fallen into unwelcome roles and are unfairly expected to take responsibility for the lion's share of domestic tasks. Others may feel social pressure to assume *less* traditionally female roles or that gender equality simply means being more like men.

Male behaviours have traditionally, and medically, been treated as the standard by which normal is judged. So whilst traits like strength and competitiveness may be valued in men, and even expected, they are disparaged in women who are simultaneously required instead to be softer and more submissive. Because these are not seen as traditional masculine traits, they are not treated as normal, inevitably positioning women as less than men.

Early psychiatry treated *women*'s neuroses, which may have been simply their expression of frustration with the **double bind** created by gender dichotomy. Even Masters and Johnson's Human Sexual Response Cycle, discussed in Chapter 2, was based on male responses, such as a steady build-up of sexual excitement, though women's sexual response is much less predictable than men's. Similarly, acts like showing emotion have been suppressed in men and associated with women, whilst still not being considered normal. This has led to the restraint of behaviours which don't suit the socially acceptable narrative. Protection of male characteristics and the associated social control of women ultimately led to development of the feminist movement.

In some social groups, an acceptable narrative is to confound expectations. For instance, there has recently been a surge in young women deliberately adopting sexually predatory behaviours they consider male in response to feeling sexually objectified. While many find this entirely positive, incredibly empowering and fun, for others the sense of objectification remains and they may use therapy to explore this further. Often, they're seeking validation: since men *seem* to derive satisfaction from having a large number of no-strings sexual partners, why shouldn't women's self-esteem be similarly boosted? For many it is, but for others validation still comes with achievement of cultural expectations such as a partner and family, often as well as a lucrative job. Recently, this has led to a number of femininity coaches vlogging and posting on social media as well as offering sessions in real life. Their message is that, to find a husband, women must suppress masculine traits and enhance feminine ones. This is nothing new, but it's now framed as female empowerment rather than wiliness or a way to achieve social fulfilment. Therapists are seeing more couples who've met this way and are experiencing difficulties when they don't live up to their unrealistic expectations of each other.

PASSING

Femininity coaches also work with trans women on the development of mannerisms, voice and makeup to enable them to pass as female. Passing, or *stealth*, is very important to some trans men and women to confirm who they are, prevent embarrassment and distress when mistakes are made and to keep them safe, especially as many are subject to verbal abuse and violence. However, other trans people begrudge being expected to pass, resenting a perceived requirement to be super-feminine in ways that cis women often are not. It's also not possible to know how someone identifies just from their appearance, so it's important that therapists don't make assumptions or question their clients' choices.

Ambiguity about gender and sexuality may sometimes be safer than passing, especially for trans women who may need to work out when and how to come out to partners. Their reactions may not be predictable, but waiting longer to get to know someone better before coming out may seem unethical.

IDENTIFYING AS TRANSVESTITE

Dressing in the opposite gender, either publicly, privately or for performance, can be considered transvestite but doesn't necessarily reflect sexuality or gender identity. Though some people find this sexually arousing, for others it's purely an identity issue. Straight, cis people may identify as transvestite or have a related fetish, such as an interest in stockings, high heels or hair.

Clients may reveal transvestite behaviours during sex therapy assessment or couples present when hidden behaviour has been discovered. Partners often don't know what to make of it and may assume they're with someone who has all along been gay or transgender. Many are able to accommodate the transvestite interests in their relationship, but some see it as deception from which it's difficult to recover. Sometimes the transvestite partner is so relieved their secret is out that they underestimate the effect on the other, who may need considerable support to catch up and understand.

COSPLAY

Costumed play involves dressing and, as closely as possible, adopting the behaviour and mannerisms of a fictional character. In Japan, where cosplay originated, characters from anime and manga are popular, often taking place at cartoon conventions. In the UK cosplay may be used as a way to express gender diversity, and is often known as *crossplay* when people portray a different gender. Cartoons are less popular than science fiction, movie characters and personalities from novels.

Slash fiction is a form of fandom whereby people, often of the same sex, pair unlikely characters in sexual situations – imagine Snape/Dumbledore from the Harry Potter books or Jean Valjean/ Javert from *Les Miserables*. Stories are often written or drawn, but couples can also act out their slash fantasy scenes using cosplay.

IDENTIFYING AS TRANSGENDER

Trans refers to all forms of gender identity which are different to the gender assigned at birth, and does not necessarily reflect sexual interest. For instance, a trans woman may be attracted only to cis men, cis women, trans men, trans women or everyone. They may also identify as non-binary, gender fluid or expansive rather than a binary gender. They don't need to have undergone any form of physical change, and it shouldn't be assumed they wish to. They also don't *need* any form of legal documentation in order to be recognised in their trans identity and to obtain documents such as a driving licence and passport. They can, however, apply for a Gender Recognition Certificate which gives them the full rights of their expressed gender and a new birth certificate. However, the process is intrusive, binary, can take several months and there's a fee. Applicants must provide evidence of living in their 'acquired' gender for at least two years. This can take the form of bank statements, payslips and a passport. They also need to have a medical diagnosis of gender dysphoria and a report from a medical professional outlining any treatment. In addition, they need a statutory declaration that they intend to live in the acquired gender for the rest of their lives and the agreement of their partner if they're married. The application is submitted to a Gender Recognition Panel who never meet the applicant. As mentioned earlier (page 106), the government reneged on a promise to allow people to self-identify as trans rather than go through the lengthy palaver of proving their commitment, affecting a great many people. According to government figures, up to half a million people identify as trans in the UK. This figure could be higher, as it may reflect binary transition rather than more nuanced identities where medical intervention isn't sought.

Those who seek medical help to affirm their gender can experience lengthy waits for NHS treatment. Currently, there are seven gender identity clinics in England, a mere four in Scotland, one in Northern Ireland and none in Wales. However, some people begin hormone treatment before attending a clinic.

CHILDREN

There's a difference between children who show an interest in non-traditional toys or activities and those who are convinced their gender has been misassigned. Families which tease, dismiss or ridicule their emotions create shame and drive feelings underground, possibly creating years of distress until they feel able to express what they've experienced.

Parents sometimes approach sex therapists for advice about how to manage gender dysphoria in their children. Many therapists have little relevant experience, but can helpfully suggest allowing the child to explore their feelings openly. Parents may be concerned about bullying and wish to protect their child, but their loving support will help the child to discover whether their feelings are as strong and lasting as they supposed.

Children can't receive hormone blockers before the age of 16 without court approval and will need the support of the Gender Identity Development Service (https://gids.nhs.uk). Children are usually referred by the family GP but other agencies, or even teachers, can refer. It may be appropriate to delay puberty with hormone therapy to give children more time.

THERAPY WITH TRANS CLIENTS

If clients have a Gender Recognition Certificate, or are in the process of applying for one, it's illegal to reveal their gender status to anyone else. It's obviously good practice to maintain confidentiality regardless, but this does mean you shouldn't really reveal gender details to your supervisor without the client's permission unless this is absolutely crucial to the work.

People can have very different attitudes to gender affirmation surgery, so don't assume they want surgery or that they've had surgery. Sometimes, treatment quickly provides confidence and sufficient sense of change for someone to continue comfortably with their existing genitals, whether they ignore them or continue to have sex with them. Other trans clients may find all or some body features distressing. For instance, some trans women are not concerned about having male genitals while others are very distressed by their penis and testicles. Some want to have a functional neovagina whilst others are content with an aesthetic vulva without a vagina. There are numerous procedures available, some involving genital surgery and others concerned with enhancing femininity, such as reducing the Adam's apple or recontouring the jawline.

Similarly, many trans men bind their breasts while they wait for **top surgery**, but some are comfortable with breasts and make no effort to hide them. Some trans men have surgery to construct male genitalia and undergo removal of reproductive organs. Often, though, it's the top surgery that's most important, perhaps with hormone therapy to deepen the voice and produce more body hair. Some trans men delay treatment until they've had children, so they can carry their own babies and chestfeed them.

Treatment frequently provides terrific relief and a sense of someone becoming who they really are, but it can sometimes be disappointing, particularly if self-image conflicts with reality. For instance, someone tall with large hands and feet won't achieve a dream of becoming willowy and petite as a result of genital surgery or hormone treatment.

It's been common to lose friends and family members during the transition process, either because they don't want to stay in touch and are unsupportive or because their reaction is disappointingly lacking in understanding. However, coming out now may be less dramatic than it once was when people were required to attempt passing in order to qualify for treatment. This could have huge and traumatic implications for employment and relationships.

Even those who simply tell others how they identify may find the experience highly emotional. It's been likened to a second or 'real' adolescence, with mood swings, impulsivity and varying degrees of outness. Hormone treatments may contribute to this, but the personal impact shouldn't be underestimated. There's a huge amount of practical repacking of life up until this point, for instance. Those who do wish to pass in their identified gender may find this denies their struggle and the relationships they've forged beforehand. They may be uncertain who to tell, what to do with earlier photographs, how and whether to choose a new name, whether to seek a Gender Recognition Certificate, whether to come out with their sexuality as well as their gender, and so on ....

COMING OUT

Coming out with a marginalised GSRD is often thought of as a rite of passage. However, it's not a single event which is then done and dusted, but an ongoing process. This is particularly the case for those who identify as bisexual or asexual, and also for those with any kind of fluid identity or who discover an unexpected attraction.

Though it can be enormously significant, coming out is sometimes taken for granted and not considered a big deal, particularly among those who've grown up knowing a number of people with diverse sexual and gender identities. On the other hand, coming out may be considered straight/cis or white privilege, as many people don't have to come out when their GSRD is the assumed 'norm'. Moreover, many people come from communities or families where coming out would be unthinkable or even dangerous.

For some, it's a struggle or confusing to come to terms with their identity and they may seek therapy for support during this time. Once they feel more secure in the way they identify, some people want to tell everyone straight away and may need help to plan this. It's not the therapist's role to encourage nor discourage coming out, but it may be helpful for the client to think through the process, who to tell first and what they're hoping will result. This may ultimately feel more controlled than rushing headlong into disclosures which are randomly shared. Often, friends and family know already, but it can be harder for people who come out for the first time later in life. Therapy can provide considerable relief and affirmation which may not exist in other contexts.

Sometimes elderly relatives choose not to acknowledge what is obvious. This can be complicated if a partner who has always been out is exerting pressure to be acknowledged themselves or wanting someone to come out globally. They may not be able to appreciate difficulties their partner is acutely aware of. For instance, occasionally work colleagues or friends feel positioned differently by the news, as if knowing and liking a gay/bi person implies they too could be gay. As therapists, we may believe this kind of homophobia has disappeared, as we may come across it much less in our own work and social environments. Again, we need to pay attention to clients' own experiences. Those who've felt unable to express their identity until now may need to express grief for what they've missed or anger that they've felt unable to be honest. Some may still be affected by traumatic events, when they were bullied or abused, which closed down their identity development.

COMING OUT TO A PARTNER

Another issue for some clients who've been in straight relationships may be how to come out to their partner and children, who may be hugely shocked and disbelieving. Therapy can do much to help someone prepare for the initial conversation with a partner and to help the couple find a way to talk to their children. It can be helpful for couples to do this together in an age-appropriate way, and to inform teachers and potentially supportive others. Studies suggest children have less problem with a parent transitioning than they do with conflict at home.

It's important to tell children as much as possible about changes that will affect them. Most significant change occurs when parents are separating, but many families do stay together. Either way, avoiding parental conflict is the best way to maintain good relationships between the entire family. Though older children may find adjustment difficult, there's evidence that relationships between both parents and their older children often improve.

Some partners are angry, feeling duped and hurt, perhaps now believing the whole relationship has been a sham, and just want to shame and humiliate. Couples can be seen together and separately to assist in coming to terms with what's happening and what will happen to their relationship now. Many split up, but remain good friends and are able to co-parent successfully. After all, the relationship was enabling enough to allow the gay partner's sexuality to evolve. But some straight partners can't get beyond their pain, fear they will be judged as sexually lacking and refuse joint therapy. They may be better referred to someone else who hasn't met the gay partner.

THERAPEUTIC ISSUES

THERAPIST SELF-DISCLOSURE

Whether or not therapists should reveal their own sexuality to their clients is contentious. Some believe they should be a blank slate and reveal nothing about themselves, so that clients can project what they need onto them. Others feel equally strongly that it's unethical not to come out to clients. Some therapists automatically disclose their sexuality, but it may not always be helpful. For instance, if someone doesn't feel gay enough, has been accused of sitting on the fence by being bisexual, has internalised homophobia or for any reason feels threatened by other gay folk, they may not be reassured. They'll probably assume a pink therapist is gay, but in other settings they may even be hoping for a straight therapist.

Of course you can discuss what to do on a case by case basis with colleagues and your supervisor, but it's important to decide in advance what you'll do if a client asks directly. Your response may need to be considered for every client or couple. For instance, it may be extremely helpful for a questioning young person to know that they're talking to someone who has experienced what they're currently going through. On the other hand, it may not be so useful for a gay middle-aged couple to find out that you're straight. It's important to be honest but also to know how the client thinks the information will affect the therapy, so do ask. Consider the context too. If someone has had difficulties with apparently straight health-care professionals, they may be anxious about repeating negative experiences. It's consequently worth knowing what triggered the question.

If you do disclose unprompted, it's wise to be clear about what you're hoping to get out of this, taking into account the individual needs of the client.

CONVERSION THERAPY

A YouGov survey commissioned by Stonewall found 9 per cent of those who are marginalised in relation to their GSRD aged 18 to 24 had been pressured to have reparative treatment to 'cure' their sexual or gender differences. This is happening even though all the main professional therapy organisations in the UK have signed a memorandum of understanding that members will not involve themselves with any form of conversion therapy, even if requested by clients themselves. Not only does conversion therapy not work, it's been demonstrated to cause considerable psychological damage.

Though about 5 per cent of over-25s have also been urged to undergo conversion therapy, younger people are considerably more at risk. As therapists shouldn't be offering conversion therapy under any circumstances, those who do are usually self-appointed and untrained. Sometimes, treatment simply involves prayer, but can also include violence or intimidation. Traumatic memories can sometimes emerge in sex therapy or be mentioned during the assessment process. Clients may need specialist trauma therapy to overcome these psychological consequences.

INTERSECTIONALITY

Intersectionality refers to the relationship between different contexts in an individual's experience. US legal theorist Kimberle Crenshaw, who coined the term, noted that black women's experience was considered in the same way as black men's, even though their treatment by men had a significant impact on their wellbeing. It's therefore important to consider the way different aspects of a person's experience meet and, potentially, exacerbate negative responses in others. For instance, there's evidence that people with marginalised GSRD identities experience more discrimination if they also have other 'differences', such as being a person of colour, poor or having a disability.

It also has to be recognised that people's experience of oppression changes along with their interests and contexts. So a trans student may feel marginalised while at college but be treated with respect once they've graduated to a successful career where they have influence over others. Indeed, power differences can be at the heart of much discrimination and poor treatment, something we shouldn't assume but should always be ready to investigate. Though not everyone has a tough time, trans individuals are at high risk of suicidality and mental health problems due to their difficulties in being recognised and accessing support, as well as outright oppression.

DISCRIMINATION

Homophobia and transphobia remain. Around half of trans people report experiencing some form of hate crime, as well as difficulties finding housing, being served in shops and eating out. Again, around half have reported disguising their identity at work following physical assault, and around a quarter have experienced domestic abuse. We need to be aware of *micro-aggressions* too, so that we're careful not to use them ourselves and take seriously incidents our clients report. Examples would include someone telling a colleague who identifies as gay that he 'obviously' likes musicals or a trans woman that she's lucky she doesn't have to pay for tampons.

PINK THERAPY

Pink therapies are those run by and for people with marginalised GSRD identities. This can be especially helpful for those who've experienced judgement or problems with other therapists or health care professionals, or found they couldn't appreciate their issues. Not all pink therapists/agencies offer sex therapy, but most have specialist training to work with identity and relationship issues. Occasionally, therapists will not themselves identify as having marginalised sexuality or gender but should have considerable experience and specialist training.

COMPASSION FOCUSED THERAPY

Clinical psychologist Paul Gilbert developed Compassion Focused Therapy as a reaction to the negative and shame-fuelled responses many people have to self-care or the interest and empathy of others. Despite longing for acceptance and understanding, many people lack the experience to manage it as they're so focused on the threat posed by others. This may be exacerbated in those who've experienced self-doubt and criticism, if not oppression, around their identity. Even those of us who take identity for granted often feel not good enough or are unable to manage painful emotions, so those who feel different may have even more difficulty in managing their self-worth and self-validating.

Therapy uses practical mindfulness approaches and CBT to improve awareness of threat sensitivity, beliefs about others and how they're perceived by them and their own self-image. Individuals are helped to manage the sometimes overwhelming emotions activated when empathy and kindness are shown to them, so they're ultimately able to offer compassion to themselves. Overcoming self-hatred and impossibly perfectionist expectations allows confidence and self-efficacy to develop.

Compassion focused approaches are helpful in all areas of health care and are used by many therapists working with shame, trauma, threat and low self-worth, which are so often experienced by those who feel, or are treated as, different.

THERAPISTS' APPROACH

However we identify, most therapists and health professionals are rightly concerned about causing offence, and keenly aware that it's impossible to know everything about every identity. This is so emotive and personal that it's impossible to get it right all the time, but we can keep talking to colleagues, teachers, supervisors and clients to share our knowledge and our mistakes. This sort of concern has led to more recent research and interest in the areas of sexuality and gender, as well as social change, which make it difficult to keep up with the pace of developments. Indeed, by the time you're reading this book, there will be even more to discover. It's important not to avoid these areas because we fear making mistakes, but to do our best and keep checking how we're doing as much as possible. Though we shouldn't expect our clients to be responsible for educating us, we can ask how they're finding therapy, what's working and what isn't. We should really get into the habit of doing this with all clients.

CHAPTER SUMMARY

- Sexuality is complex and changeable, but is often defined by popular ideas that many people can't relate to.
- Straight cisgender people may not give much consideration to their sexual or gender identity, which leaves them more open to absorbing societal rules about how they should behave.
- Meanwhile, many people feel marginalised because their sexuality and/or gender experience doesn't conform to these rules.
- Therapy can assist people to discover what works for them.

FURTHER READING

Barker, M-J. (2019) *Gender, Sexual, and Relationship Diversity (GSRD)*, Lutterworth: BACP: bacp-gender-sexual-relationship-diversity-gpacp001-april19. pdf. Accessed August 21, 2021.

Barker, M-J. (2018) *Rewriting the Rules: An Anti Self-Help Guide to Love, Sex and Relationships*, 2nd edn, Abingdon: Routledge.

Barker, M-J. & Iantaffi, A. (2019) *Life Isn't Binary: On Being Both, Beyond, and In-Between*, London: Jessica Kingsley.

Beattie, M. & Leniham, P. (2018) *Counselling Skills for Working with Gender Diversity and Identity*, London: Jessica Kingsley.

Chen, A. (2021) *Ace: What Asexuality Reveals about Desire, Society, and the Meaning of Sex*, Boston, MA: Beacon Press.

Fosse, M.J. (2021) *The Many Faces of Polyamory*, New York: Routledge.

Gilbert, P. (2009) Introducing compassion-focused therapy, *Advances in Psychiatric Treatment*, 15, 199–208.

Hardy, J.W. & Easton, D. (2017) *The Ethical Slut*, 3rd edn, Berkeley, CA: Ten Speed Press.

Kincel, A. (2021) *Exploring Masculinity, Sexuality, and Culture in Gestalt Therapy: An Autoethnography*, Abingdon: Routledge.

Muldoon, M. & Hernandez, W. (2022) *A Quick and Easy Guide to Asexuality*, Portland, OR: Oni Press.

Richards, C. & Barrett, J. (2021) *Trans and Non-binary Gender Healthcare for Psychiatrists, Psychologists and Other Healthcare Professionals*, Cambridge, UK: Cambridge University Press.

Silva, T. (2021) *Still Straight: Sexual Flexibility Among White Men in Rural America*, New York: New York University Press.

Witt, E. (2018) *Future Sex: A New Kind of Free Love*, London: Faber & Faber.

RESOURCES

Chemsex support: www.dean.st/chemsex-care-plan/.

Galop (for GSRD marginalised victims of abuse): http://www.galop.org.uk/. Freephone 0800 999 5428

Gender Identity Research & Education Society (GIRES): www.gires. org.uk.

It's A Sin (C4 series about AIDS in the 1980s): www.channel4.com/programmes/ its-a-sin.

National Domestic Violence Helpline: Freephone 0808 247

Pink Therapy: https://pinktherapy.com.

Polyamory UK: www.polyamory.org.uk.

The Book of Polyamory, BBC Radio 4: www.bbc.co.uk/programmes/m000gkw9.

The Urgency of Intersectionality (TED Talk by Kimberle Crenshaw): www. ted.com/talks/kimberle_crenshaw_the_urgency_of_intersectionality.

Stonewall (Information Service for GSRD identifying people): www.stonewall. org.uk/help-advice/contact-stonewalls-information-service Freephone 0800 050 2020 info@stonewall.org.uk.

BIBLIOGRAPHY

Bachmann, C.L. & Gooch, B. (2018) *LGBT in Britain Health Report*, London: Stonewall.

Bridges, T. & Pascoe, C. J. (2014) Hybrid masculinities: New directions in the sociology of men and masculinities, *Sociology Compass*, 8(3), 246–258.

Foucault, M. (2020) *The History of Sexuality Volume 1: The Will to Knowledge*, London: Penguin Random House.

Government Equalities Office (2018) *Trans People in the UK*, London: GOV. UK. Accessed January 2, 2022.

Moskowitz, D.A., Turrubiates, J. & Lozano, H. (2013) Physical, behavioral, and psychological traits of gay men identifying as bears, *Archives of Sexual Behaviour*, 42, 775–784.

Niki, D. (2018) Now you see me, now you don't: addressing bisexual invisibility in relationship therapy. *Sexual and Relationship Therapy*, 33(1–2),45–57.

Quidley-Rodriguez, N. & De Santis, J.P. (2017) A literature review of health risks in the bear community, a gay subculture, *American Journal of Men's Health*, 11(6), 1673–1679.

Richards, C. & Barker, M. (2013) *Sexuality & Gender for Mental Health Professionals: A Practical Guide*, London: Sage.

Ward, J. (2008) Dude-sex: White masculinities and 'authentic' heterosexuality among dudes who have sex with dudes, *Sexualities*, 11(4), 414–434.

SPECIALIST AREAS

Sex and relationship therapy is a vast area, making it difficult to be aware of every presentation and currently topical issue. This chapter aims to offer the basics of some areas you may meet, with ideas about how to find further information. Some of the topics aren't really that specialist, but may not be encountered that often.

DEPENDENCY ASSOCIATED ISSUES

Many people use sex to manage their mood. Indeed, this is sometimes encouraged, as sex can be relaxing and an orgasm resets the body and produces feel-good endorphins. Problems can, however, develop when someone needs sex to feel normal.

PORN DEPENDENCY

In the past, viewing pornographic images was a lot more trouble. People had to go to a cinema, hire a video, buy magazines or visit a sex show. Now pornography can be viewed anywhere on internet devices. With tablets, laptops and smartphones, someone's porn source can be in their pocket. It's also very easy to spend hours on the internet, and the click-load buzz as we anticipate what will come up keeps us clicking again and again. There's some evidence that this process can hook us as we produce hormones like dopamine, which makes us enjoy ourselves and want to repeat the experience, and vasopressin which makes us concentrate more. Oxytocin, known as 'the cuddle hormone', is released during partnered sex and has a

DOI: 10.4324/9781003265641-6

bonding effect, which may be why couples get along a little better for a few days after making love.

The problem with excessive porn use is that watching produces an abundance of oxytocin and a warm sense of wellbeing. This is desirable as an occasional fix, but when people use porn as a reward at the end of a long day, or rely on it to self-soothe, they can sometimes end up needing more and more extreme images to achieve the same effect. Eventually, partnered sex can stop being stimulating enough, which sometimes leads people to seek exciting real life encounters with sex workers, strangers they meet or through hook-ups. Couples may also seek sex therapy to deal with issues like ED or delayed ejaculation, so it's always worth asking how much porn clients are accessing.

Individuals may present with concerns about their porn habits or sexual behaviour. Often a couple will present when someone's behaviour has been recently discovered and the partner is in shock. The deception involved can feel like an affair which some relationships can't survive, particularly when the user continues to deny what they're doing. However, partners should be discouraged from making rash decisions, such as leaving or telling other people what's happened. They may need considerable support for some time, especially if the behaviour predates the relationship, as they may feel repositioned and that the relationship was never as they thought. Some try to change the affected partner's behaviour by offering sex or by policing their internet use, but neither really work. The person needs to take responsibility for their own behaviour and also to manage their own change process. In any case, the behaviour isn't about sex but about using it to self-soothe.

Sometimes there isn't really a problem. Partners may object to masturbation, for instance, or aren't that interested in sex and want a therapist to support them in this. Working non-judgementally with any underlying trauma and coaching in strategies to self-regulate are crucial whilst the client attempts to reduce or stop the behaviours and replace them with less damaging strategies. There are several support groups and specialist therapists who have been trained to work with sexual dependency. However, the idea that sex can be addictive is controversial, as it has been used as a way of demonising some sexual behaviours, especially by fundamentalist religious groups. Nonetheless, sex therapists are seeing people who have started to find their porn use problematic. Often, they seek help when they progress to watching increasingly more extreme images to get the same buzz, or to real life encounters they would never have imagined themselves considering in the past. While some people don't find their behaviour a problem and don't want to change, some feel enormous shame and become trapped in a cycle of using sex to manage the shame and then feeling even worse.

It's not only pornography that can be a problem. Use of chat rooms, cybersex, constantly checking hook-up apps, phone sex, sexting, seeking multiple partners and use of sex workers are among other activities which may eventually cause difficulties in some people.

PARAPHILIAS AND OFFENDING

Paraphilia usually refers to pleasure in unusual sex, but it's not really clear what unusual means. One person's turn off is another's delight. Working with offending is a specialist area, and most sex therapists are unlikely to be involved. However, they may see couples who are recovering from discovery of an offending behaviour or an arrest. Obviously, sex with minors comes into this category, as does rape and sexual assault, but we more commonly encounter behaviours such as *dogging*. This involves watching or being watched having sex, often in cars parked in lay-bys or woodland. Other common behaviours include non-consensual touch or *frotteurism*, when someone rubs their body against someone non-consenting, often in a crowd; exposing oneself or *exhibitionism*; and sexual harassment, which includes sending images or messages which aren't wanted.

ANABOLIC STEROIDS

It's often worth asking about use of anabolic steroids when apparently fit clients present with recently acquired body changes or ED which occurs both during partnered sex and masturbation. Both men and women use anabolic steroids, administered by injection, creams, or tablets, which produce the effects of the hormone testosterone, improving body mass and sports performance and promoting quicker healing following injuries. Their use often begins in young people who have issues with body image and may have been bullied. There's some evidence of an association with sexual assault in women, though this is equivocal.

Because they can have a damaging effect on the body, particularly on sex and reproduction, anabolic steroids are not available without a prescription, and it's illegal to sell or give them to anyone else. Unwanted effects in men include ED and shrivelled testicles, low sperm count, breast development, baldness, body pains and increased risk of prostate cancer. In women they can cause clitoral enlargement, loss of breast tissue, menstrual issues and a deep voice. Loss of head hair, but growth in facial and body hair, may also be experienced. Some report an increased libido. Both men and women can experience severe skin problems, mental health difficulties, mood swings and aggression.

Despite their harmful effects, many users believe they have control because they take breaks in use, or switch brands, but harmful effects remain, including cardiovascular, liver and kidney disease. It can be extremely dangerous to cease use suddenly, so users tend to reduce the dose rather than stop. Anabolic steroids are also addictive, especially to women, so may be difficult to give up anyway.

Sometimes individuals present for sex therapy hoping that another cause will be found for their sexual problems, or that the therapist will have a fix. In couples where anabolic steroid use hasn't been suspected or revealed, therapists may be baffled about why therapy isn't progressing. Couples often present when one partner is worried about the other's use or their health and sexual relationship. Much of the work may consequently involve repairing the relationship and supporting partners who are unable to persuade the other to change.

SEXUALLY TRANSMITTED AND GENITAL INFECTIONS

Unless you work in a specialist clinic or urology department, you probably won't need to know a great deal about sexually transmitted infections (STIs). However, because people often don't like to admit having them, they're rarely discussed and may be brought up by clients seeking information. We're also seeing more clients who assume STIs aren't relevant to them, so they don't need to have checks. Some have picked up the message that barrier methods of contraception prevent STIs, rather than that they help to prevent them. People returning to dating following a long relationship are sometimes out of touch with the potential risks or safer sex messages. For instance, they may not use condoms as they're postmenopausal. It's also worth checking that clients understand some STIs can be symptomless and that they can recognise symptoms if they do occur. These may include painful sex or abdominal pain, discharge from the penis, vagina or urethra, pain weeing, soreness, redness and itching. Women may experience spotting following intercourse or between periods. Any of these symptoms should be checked out – clients should be advised not to wait to develop them all and not to ignore them if they're mild.

The majority of STIs can be treated and forgotten, but this wasn't always the case and some have longer-term consequences. It's important if you're sexually active to have regular checks at a sexual health clinic, especially if you or a regular partner are having sex with more than one person. Some infections don't show up immediately, appear to go away, or some people don't have any symptoms.

Though this is fairly rare, some STIs, such as scabies, can be transmitted non-sexually too, sometimes just by close contact. As well as having regular checks, using barrier contraception, washing and drying sex toys thoroughly after use, and not sharing them, clients should advise sexual partners if they develop symptoms or are diagnosed with a STI.

BACTERIAL INFECTIONS

These are normally successfully treated with antibiotics. *Chlamydia* is an example of a very common STI which responds well to penicillin. However, it's reported to have no symptoms in two-thirds of women and half of men. If left untreated it can cause scarring of reproductive organs and pelvic inflammatory disease (PID). This may be painful or symptomless, and is sometimes only discovered when someone has problems with fertility. There is a national screening programme for under-25-year-olds as it's the most common STI in young people. *Mycoplasma* is similar to chlamydia, but less common and a bit harder to treat, as it's more resistant to penicillin. Several checks may be needed to be sure that it's cleared up.

Gonorrhoea is almost as common as chlamydia but is more widely spread across age groups. Though it can usually be successfully treated with a single antibiotic injection, it can have serious consequences if left. It can sometimes lead to PID, for example, and can be passed to the foetus in pregnancy, sometimes causing blindness. Half of women have no symptoms.

Syphilis begins with symptoms which may be mild and then disappear, including painless sores or skin tags on the genitals and anus, a red rash on the body, including hands and feet, a temperature or swollen glands. If left untreated, symptoms may come and go over many years, silently causing damage to the brain, major organs and joints. Pregnant women are screened for syphilis as it can infect the baby. If caught early, it's usually treated with a single injection of penicillin. Otherwise, treatment may take longer and there may be more damage the longer it's left.

A runny greyish discharge and smell of rotten fish, especially associated with sex, suggests infection with *bacterial vaginosis* (BV). This is not a STI, and can affect all women, but can be passed between women during sex. BV occurs when the normal bacteria in the vagina become disrupted for some reason, and it can recur after antibiotic treatment. Half of women have no symptoms but it can increase the risk of other infections, particularly chlamydia.

VIRUSES

Genital warts are caused by the *human papilloma virus* (HPV). They can be quite tricky to eliminate, sometimes requiring several months of specialist treatment, and can return. Use of condoms, female condoms and dental dams can help prevent spread, and 12–13-year-olds are offered a vaccination which also helps prevent cervical cancer. Some older people may be offered a vaccination, including anyone who is immunosuppressed and men who have sex with men.

Genital herpes can be passed on through any contact with an infected area and remains in the body permanently. Most of the time it's dormant, but during outbreaks the person develops blisters which burst to leave raw painful areas. The blisters may be inside the mouth, throat, vagina or anus as well as on the skin, but someone can be infectious without symptoms. The whole genital area may shed infection without symptoms so, though helpful, barriers like condoms don't always prevent spread. Sometimes the blisters don't appear until long after someone has been infected and outbreaks can occur many times, though the first is usually the most severe. Some people have so many outbreaks that they need antiviral medication on a long-term basis, especially anyone who is immunosuppressed. Flare-ups can be treated with local anaesthetic such as Lidocaine. There are some dating apps specially for people affected by herpes.

PARASITES

Trichomoniasis has a characteristic fishy smell and may produce a frothy yellow or green discharge in women and a thin white one in men. It's caused by a parasite which inhabits the urethra and vagina and usually clears up after a week of treatment.

Pubic lice can be a real nuisance as they can infect any hairy area apart from the head, and are spread through close physical contact. Though they're small and may be difficult to see, infection is often evident, as they leave droppings in the pants that look like black powder and cause soreness and itching. They can cause eye infections if they attach to the lashes. They're usually easily removed with an insecticide shampoo or lotion, repeated after a week.

Scabies mites burrow under the skin, causing intense itching and a rash, and can be passed on by any physical contact. Symptoms may not appear for a few weeks, so it's important to inform sexual contacts from the past two or three months. Red spots between the fingers are usually the earliest symptoms. Treatment is usually with an ointment or lotion that has to be applied to the whole body and repeated after a week.

YEAST INFECTION

Thrush is not a STI but it can be transmitted sexually. Partners can unknowingly cause reinfection, so they should really be treated too. The main symptom is intense itching, and there may be white patches on the skin which wipe off to leave raw areas. It can be treated with over-the-counter pessaries, creams and oral tablets. If it doesn't clear up quickly, however, it does need to be medically checked, as the itching may be caused by something else rather than, or as well as, thrush. Over-treating can also produce thrush-like symptoms, so it's always best to seek medical advice about a persistent or severe infection.

HIV

Human immunodeficiency virus (HIV) can be spread sexually, via dirty or used needles, from mother to child in the womb, during labour, or while breastfeeding. If left untreated it can lead to *acquired immune deficiency syndrome* (AIDS), when the body's defences become overwhelmed and susceptible to a variety of illnesses. Though HIV doesn't leave the body, antiretroviral drugs can be used to repair the immune system and reduce the virus so much that's it's undetectable. Someone who thinks they could have been exposed to HIV can get post-exposure prophylaxis (PEP) from accident and emergency departments or sexual health clinics. It has to be started within 72 hours of exposure and continued for a month. Pre-exposure prophylaxis (PREP) should also now be available from sexual health clinics to help reduce the risk of infection to the individual and their partner(s). However, recreational drug users with HIV may have more difficulty clearing the drugs from their systems or they may reduce the effectiveness of HIV medication.

ED is relatively common among men with HIV, particularly as they grow older. This is often due to low testosterone, to some drug interactions, to the effect of HIV on the cardiovascular system or there may be psychological causes. The drug regime, side effects and need to follow a healthy life can take its toll on some people, who feel very different and that their future is uncertain despite the effectiveness of treatment. ED is usually treated with testosterone and PDE 5 inhibitors, but work on any identity issues or relationship difficulties can be helpful, as can sensate focus if ED is persistent. Some people have body issues, as abdominal fat and prominent veins can be a problem. Solution focused therapy approaches can be helpful when someone prefers only brief engagement with therapy. A useful goal is to improve feelings of control.

RELATIONAL AREAS

TANTRIC SEX

Tantric sex is an ancient Hindu practice, which is often regarded as a bit mysterious. Some therapists are even rather suspicious about it. However, much sex therapy practice has its basis in tantric approaches. It's mindful, aiming to slow down the sexual experience and urging lovers to be in the moment. As in sensate focus, lovers are encouraged to focus on their own experience and to spend time getting to know their own and their partner's whole body. There's considerable emphasis on preparing the environment too, attending to all the senses, just as we may ask clients to prepare the room for sensate focus experiments.

It's all about the journey rather than the outcome, so orgasm isn't the focus of tantric sex. Rather, the emphasis is on learning and developing the relationship with oneself and one's partner. Sexual psychologist Dr David Schnarch borrowed the tantric idea of gazing into each other's eyes and keeping the eyes open more often during sex. Psychotherapist Wendy Maltz advises couples where one or both partners are affected by trauma to use a tantric hands-on-hearts exercise. Partners sit opposite each other with their hands on each other's chest, sending messages of love and appreciation through their bodies into each other's hearts. This is often used with gazing as a pre-sensate experiment. As much as possible, partners are encouraged to synchronise and slow their breathing.

SEX TOYS

Most people probably try a sex toy at some point, whether this is to assist with solo sex or for play with a partner. There is a vast range of toys available for all kinds of sex, some as props or aesthetic enhancers and many to facilitate orgasm or sexual comfort. There are specialist toys for people with limited mobility to help them masturbate, as well as equipment to assist with positioning for partnered sex. Some sex therapists ask clients to experiment with choosing a toy or even just looking at some online. Couples with little experience, or who need help to normalise being sexual, particularly benefit from this. Some partners object to the use of toys as they have strong beliefs about 'giving' their partner a sexual experience themselves. Sex toys may need to be reframed as a fun enhancement for both partners, and work may be needed to help the partner focus more on their own experience rather than feeling so much responsibility to satisfy the other.

SEXOMNIA

This is a sleep disorder in which someone wakes to find themselves having sex. This can cause serious relationship problems if partners believe they're conscious and knowingly taking advantage of them, particularly if they've recently declined sexual contact. Sometimes, though, it's the apparently unaffected partner who actually has sexomnia, and the partner who seems to have initiated the contact is actually responding.

Couples often present to baffled GPs and sex therapists who may also assume what's happening is abusive. Thankfully, however, the condition is gradually becoming better understood. While therapy can help repair their relationship, the couple also need reassurance that this is not a sexual disorder and that it can be successfully treated at a sleep clinic.

FANTASY

Some couples see sexual fantasy as a betrayal of their partner, especially if it involves imagining sex with someone else. However, some people actually find too much emphasis on their partner off-putting during sex, as it makes them more self-conscious or anxious. Fantasy can shift the emphasis enough to overcome this.

Fantasy is often extremely helpful for those who have difficulty orgasming to help them focus their own experience rather than worrying about what their partner is thinking or feeling. Couples often enjoy creating and sharing fantasies, but masturbatory fantasies are often better kept to oneself as partners' reactions can easily spoil them.

Some couples like to extend their fantasy into role play, sometimes using props or dressing up. Pretending to be someone else can be especially helpful for people who feel embarrassed or guilty about sex. This is frequently a result of negative messages received growing up, so occupying a range of characters can help to normalise sexual pleasure.

Though by no means all role play or fantasy is violent, some people like to imagine being forced into sex. This doesn't usually mean they want to be sexually abused in real life. Rather, they may have received negative messages about sexual pleasure and enjoy sex more if they role play or fantasise that sex isn't their choice.

KINK

Role play, fetishes, and BDSM are often considered forms of kink, which is really anything someone sees as not **vanilla sex**. Some couples stray into BDSM, and should be advised to check out websites or literature which explain safe practice and how to find suitable equipment. There's considerable information available, as well as porn, dating websites, shops and information for people with disabilities or who are older. Engaging in kink is rarely the issue couples bring to therapy, so is usually something to be aware of rather than to address.

BDSM

BDSM play usually involves role playing, and it's important couples are clear about their roles and the stories they're enacting. They need to have safe words that mean stop, as 'no' and 'stop' may not mean this in the context of the story or 'scene'. The BDSM community may mention *Risk Accepted Consensual Kink (RACK)*, which acknowledges that injury is possible. However, it's worth being aware that consent is not a defence for actual bodily harm in the UK. Though it rarely happens, people have been prosecuted both for causing harm and for abetting it by consenting.

Many people experience pain associated with a highly pleasurable altered state of consciousness or spirituality. Aftercare is also an important part of BDSM, when the dominant partner cares for the submissive. Some therapists find this difficult to come to terms with, assuming kink is always associated with pathology. However, there are probably as many reasons why people wish to engage in BDSM as there are people who do, and research suggests their experiences are actually more consensual and 'safe'.

FETISHES

Fetishes involve the eroticising of objects, clothing or body parts so that they're often included in partnered sex or masturbation. Someone aroused by high heels may be excited by seeing or holding them, wearing them, or having sex with someone else who is wearing them, for instance.

TRAUMA

Sex therapy can be triggering for many kinds of trauma, but particularly interpersonal trauma, including domestic abuse, sexual assault and childhood neglect. Difficulties in trusting people or fear of not being good enough can lead to problems as relationships become closer. Sometimes people genuinely believe they have dealt with their trauma, don't see what happened as unusual, minimise their abuse or don't mention it in the history taking. It can then surface either as a hugely distressing trigger or more nuanced block during treatment. It can be helpful to pause therapy if this happens, while the trauma is treated. Sometimes treatment can be undertaken alongside sex therapy, but it may be more productive to concentrate on dealing with the trauma first. If it's identified in history taking, for instance, it can be worked with before starting sex therapy. EMDR and IFS therapies can both be extremely effective, particularly when used in combination. Even where sex therapists are able to offer these, some clients prefer to see a different therapist to separate their current relationship and sex therapy from what happened to them in the past. Similarly, partners of people who use sexual behaviours for mood regulation which becomes problematic may prefer to see someone different for therapy to assist their sexual reconnection. Having said this, the partners of people who have experienced trauma commonly have their own trauma history which may also need to be identified and addressed.

FEMALE GENITAL MUTILATION (FGM)

FGM refers to deliberate genital injury which has no medical justification. In some parts of the world, a variety of procedures are carried out to improve the marriageability of women and girls, including removal of the clitoris and virtual closure of the vaginal orifice and labia, making menstruation and urination extremely difficult and leading to infection. Women often have to be cut to have intercourse and give birth. According to the World Health Organization, there are more than 200 million women and girls currently affected, with more than 3 million at risk of being cut every year, including countries where the practice is illegal. There are more than 30 countries where FGM is widely practised, mainly in the Middle East, Asia and Africa, with around 137,000 women and girls in the UK thought to have undergone the procedure.

The number of UK cases appeared to drop during the pandemic, but this may have been due to families deferring pregnancy or not presenting for smear tests, so that few cases were picked up. In fact, numbers may even have risen as home schooling during lockdowns may have provided an opportunity for FGM to be practised without leaving the country. In non-Covid times, girls were often taken out of school for trips to visit relatives abroad where FGM was carried out, sometimes accompanied by marriage or betrothals.

It's often assumed that women and girls who have undergone FGM are unable to enjoy sex or have orgasms, but good sexual functioning can often be restored. The majority of the clitoris is under the skin, and even when the external clitoris has been removed the stump can often still be stimulated. Multidisciplinary clinics exist offering counselling, contraception, and remedial surgery to allow menstruation and sex. Sex therapy may also be offered, and clients increasingly present themselves for treatment in both NHS and private practices.

Often, the trauma that's been experienced needs to be treated before tackling sexual functioning. FGM is usually performed on a number of girls at the same time, often around the age of seven. Girls about to undergo the practice are often dressed in party frocks, given presents, and made to feel special, so they may have no idea of what's to come. They're held down for the procedure, often by women they trust, which can have a devastating effect on their ability to form relationships. They may be cut by older women, with little or no formal medical knowledge, without anaesthetic and using a range of instruments which can include shards of glass and razor blades. Bleeding may be profuse and is sometimes fatal.

OTHER GENITAL SURGERY

We should routinely be asking about any procedures or surgery on the genitals, as many clients now have cosmetic surgery, especially **labiaplasty**, or male circumcision. More men are now objecting to circumcision carried out in infancy and it's becoming less common.

Any genital procedure can be associated with feelings of shame or difference. With FGM, women may gain a sense of belonging in their communities, which can mitigate some of the traumatic effects. In the UK, however, women may feel more different, which may make them more open to treatment or lead them to deny they've been cut.

SHAME

For those who've had FGM, there may be shame about having had the process or shame that they're now looking for treatment. Sensitivity and openness are obviously essential to gain trust and enable the person to engage with the therapy or setting.

Avoidance of shame motivates much sexual acting out and avoidance. Sometimes people develop behaviours which create guilt rather than shame – such as an affair or sexting – as shame is about the person rather than what they do. Others are often supportive of misguided behaviours but not so sympathetic about people they consider to have overstepped the rules of their community or who have hurt others. Many people who use sexual acting out to manage their shame – and thereby create more shame – feel that whatever traumas caused it in the first place were their own fault, and that they wouldn't have been treated as they were if they were worthy or good enough. This can make it hard for them to become close to others, both because they anticipate rejection and because they fear their deficits will be discovered. Such feelings may be denied or not even be available to conscious thought.

While some people withdraw and blame themselves, others manage their shame by refusing to take responsibility and blaming others. They may develop a grandiose and entitled manner which makes therapy challenging, if they can even be persuaded to attend. However, they may respond well to therapy which is framed as in their interests, though it's important not to collude with inequality in relationships or actual abuse.

SAFEGUARDING

It's essential to be able to recognise any form of abuse in couples. This may not be obvious as abusive partners are often successful at grooming others to believe they're caring, and often accuse their victims of being abusive. Women who are being abused may present as upset and complaining while the perpetrator seems calm and sensible. Women's complaints may not be about verbal, physical, financial, sexual or emotional abuse but about not being heard or supported. Indeed, women may not realise they're experiencing abuse and may blame themselves. Men who are being abused often minimise what's happening and are protective of their partners. These presentations mean abuse can easily be missed, so it's always worth asking couples individually how they argue and resolve disagreements or manage their own and each other's bad moods, as well as directly enquiring about abusive behaviours. Go with your gut feeling if something doesn't seem right, and investigate further. Supervisors should always advise and offer support if you have concerns, as should agency case managers.

It's also often worth asking what sort of pornography someone's watching. It's surprising how often people admit to having seen images with children, or this can open up a conversation about violent porn and real life. Some people's sex education has been based on the porn they've watched and this may be normalised for both partners who sometimes think it's expected even when neither enjoys it.

TALKING TO CHILDREN ABOUT SEX

An open dialogue with children about sex and pornography makes it less likely they'll watch disturbing pornography without seeking advice. It's common to leave such conversations too late, as many children have already seen porn by the time it's mentioned at school or home. Many are also unaware of the risks associated with sharing images of body parts. *Revenge porn*, as it's colloquially known, is an offence if someone passes on an image aiming to cause distress, which non-consensual sharing can be assumed to do. They might believe they're only sharing with a single friend and not realise how fast these pictures spread.

Many parents worry about discussing sex with their children, though they usually feel they have a responsibility to do so. Some approach a sex therapist for advice when their children are approaching puberty, when they start dating or when there have been problems in school or in friendship groups. They may think of their responsibility to provide sex education in terms of a single 'birds and bees' conversation, a series of brief focused discussions or an ability to respond to questions rather than broach the subject themselves. However, conversations are much easier if sex isn't felt to be a taboo or awkward subject. Answering questions in age appropriate ways makes it easier for children to confide in their parents when they need to.

Even when children are tiny, parents can model respect for their bodies and use occasions like bath times to accurately name body parts and talk about what they do. Conversations can readily be initiated when there's a context for them, such as when a friend's mum is pregnant. Being consistent about issues like consent is important from an early age. For instance, children should never be made to hug or kiss visiting relatives if they don't want to. It can also be helpful to encourage children to have opinions and sometimes disagree with adults. Children who feel they always have to be obedient to adults, and fear being in trouble, are at much more risk from predatory others. It's always easier to discuss how to say no to unwanted touch, and have a plan for how to manage in situations where they could be at risk, when children feel comfortable talking about their bodies with their parents.

TECHNOLOGY

Technology has had a huge influence on relationships and the expectations partners have. They now have access to one another all the time, which can have significant drawbacks. A frequent complaint is that one partner doesn't answer messages immediately or takes too long, so clients often need help with self-regulation to manage the wait for a response. Significant negotiation may be needed to reach agreement about what's a reasonable amount of contact.

Couples who've split also do themselves no favours by continuing to check their ex's social media and torture themselves when it appears they're getting on with their life or seem to be happy with someone else. Some people spend a great deal of time stalking partners or people who interest them online and obsessing about the meaning of posts or the significance of messages. It's easy to misunderstand and either take offence or read much more into off-the-cuff comments than was intended. Some partners actually put surveillance equipment on the other's devices or agree to apps which monitor whereabouts. Even when constant monitoring is consensual, it can quickly start to feel stifling. Partners don't always agree to being tagged in photographs or messages either, which can lead to arguments about whether this means they've got something to hide. Constant checking of phones, even when this is work related, or playing online games, can distract from the relationship or family time, so couples may wish to set boundaries around this.

The pseudo-intimacy of online relationships can both encourage affairs and disappoint couples who met online when they get together for a date. Many persist with their relationship if the online chats were what they needed, assuming they have bonded. They may end up blaming each other for not being what they seemed.

As it's so easy for people to contact old flames or start up new relationships online, people often find themselves quickly involved. Consequently, what constitutes an affair now is very different from what clients brought a decade or two ago. Someone may have been seeking emotional support initially, but found sexual or romantic content crept in. Sometimes partners say they could understand a sexual affair but that they're even more hurt by emotional texts. Affairs are often discovered when messages are seen online, frequently when they're delivered to a tablet as well as a phone and spotted by the partner.

AFFAIRS

Upon discovery of an affair, couples often present in a state of crisis, wanting the relationship to survive but unsure how to go forward. The exception is exit affairs where one partner expected the other wouldn't tolerate infidelity, but finds they're prepared to give them another chance. It's often quickly evident there's a split agenda, with one partner wanting to work at the relationship and the other already emotionally out of it. Guilt may make them decide to try again, and they may agree to relationship or sex therapy which just keeps stalling. It's usually more helpful to focus on a common interest such as co-parenting or how to cohabit until they can move than trying to reboot the love.

Even when both partners actively want to repair the relationship, previous assumptions about how they'd feel and behave often turn out not to predict the confusing and changeable emotions they experience. Partners often want every detail of the affair, torturing themselves to think that it was happening at the same time as other life events when the couple seemed happy or they felt supported. Now they wonder if the whole relationship has been a sham. They should be advised not to dig around for information, however. Most people having an affair see it as completely separate to their family lives, and may find it hard to understand the connections their partner is making. It's also difficult to expunge images of the affair once details have been given, making it harder to move on.

Some people feel so guilty about their affair that they soak up blame to the extent that the relationship becomes unequal and punishing. Partners may feel they should keep explaining how hurt they are and feel foolish if they forgive. Forgiveness may not be possible, but acceptance may be. Couples can be helped to look forward and plan the life and relationship they both want, which can end up being closer than it was before.

NEURODIVERSITY

Conditions like *attention deficit disorder* (ADD) and autism attract considerable speculation about their impact on sexual expression, with ADD particularly implicated in erratic, impulsive and hypersexual behaviour. However, studies suggest that, when such behaviours exist, they are unlikely to be related to the ADD itself, but may be used as a way of self-regulating.

ATTENTION DEFICIT DISORDER

Difficulties concentrating and anxiety can make it hard to focus during sex, and people with ADD may also have some sensitivities, particularly skin rashes. They are hypervigilant, often expecting criticism, which can make it harder for partners to share ways to have their own needs met. Some of the medication for ADD can cause aggression and irritability, so there may be more difficulty in tolerating criticism or negative remarks. Some people who are prescribed SSRI antidepressants develop loss of desire or problems with arousal. This is worth discussing with the prescribing practitioner, as experimentation with dosage and drugs can usually overcome these issues.

AUTISTIC SPECTRUM DISORDER

Individuals affected by autism or autistic traits can experience both sexual and relationship problems as a consequence. Many have sensory sensitivities, so dislike certain kinds of touch, smells or textures. This can cause aversions to some sexual behaviours, such as oral sex, or to body parts. Some people have sensory deficits, particularly in relation to touch, so may find it more difficult to become aroused or to orgasm. Partners may feel unattractive if this becomes more obvious as the relationship's novelty or NRE wear off.

Difficulties in reading their partner's mood can exacerbate any relationship issues which arise from sexual problems. The extreme attention paid to their partner at the outset of the relationship can sooner or later be superseded by other interests, such as work, a hobby or the couple's children.

Sex therapy can be enormously helpful in providing the couple with a different experience where they learn to have their own needs met by working collaboratively to prompt and support each other.

BRAIN INJURY

Following surgery, an accident, stroke or development of a condition like dementia, some people can become sexually disinhibited, making inappropriate comments or touching their partner when this is unwelcome. Though this is often temporary, it can be distressing, especially if the affected partner is inappropriate with other people as well. Forgetfulness and irritability can also challenge relationships, particularly if the person appears physically recovered. Where they appear frail or vulnerable, sex can seem abusive to the fitter partner, although restoring intimacy may be desperately wanted by both of them. Sex therapy can be helpful in providing strategies to manage mood swings and in gradually reintroducing sexual behaviour at a pace and intensity which works for both partners.

THERAPIST RESPONSIBILITY

Though this chapter attempts to provide an overview of various issues that may come the way of sex therapists during their careers, it's practitioners' responsibility to find out about unfamiliar presentations as they arise, especially as developments in sex therapy are moving so fast.

CHAPTER SUMMARY

- Sexual dependency can occur as a result of excessive porn use, especially when used for mood management; dependent use of anabolic steroids can also affect sexual functioning.
- Sex therapists need to be aware of STIs so they can offer advice where necessary.
- They also need to be able to recognise trauma and treat or refer.
- Practitioners may encounter unfamiliar presentations and are urged to stay up to date with research as it arises.

FURTHER READING

Aston, M. (2020) *The Asperger Couple's Workbook*, 2nd edition, London: Jessica Kingsley.

Birchard, T. (2017) *Overcoming Sex Addiction: A Self-Help Guide*, Abingdon: Routledge.

Boyd, D. (2015) *It's Complicated: The Social Lives of Networked Teens*, New Haven, CT: Yale University Press.

Home Office (2019) *Female Genital Mutilation: The Facts*. www.gov.uk/gov
ernment/publications/female-genital-mutilation-leaflet. Accessed January
16, 2022.

Perel, E. (2017) *The State of Affairs: Rethinking Infidelity*, London: Yellow Kite.

Sanderson, C. (2015) *Counselling Skills for Working with Shame*, London: Jessica
Kingsley.

Shahbaz, C. & Chirinos, P. (2021) *Becoming a Kink Aware Therapist*, New
York: Routledge.

RESOURCES

Daughters of Eve (charity for those affected by FGM): www.dofeve.org/.

Fetlife (social networking website for kink interests): https://fetlife.com.

FGM with Dr Leyla Hussein, Real Sex Education Podcast: https://podcasts.
apple.com/gb/podcast/s3-7-fgm-with-dr-leyla-hussein/id1521289128?i=
1000539981416.

BIBLIOGRAPHY

Abdulcadir, J., Tille, J-C. & Petignat, P. (2017) Management of painful clitoral
neuroma after female genital mutilation/cutting, *Reproductive Health*, 14(22),
274–281.

Botter, C., Sawan, D., SidAhmed-Mezi, M., Spanopoulou, S., Luchian, S.,
Meningaud, J.P. & Hersant, B. (2021) Clitoral reconstructive surgery after
female genital mutilation/cutting: anatomy, technical innovations and
updates of the initial technique, *Journal of Sexual Medicine*, 18(5), 996–1008.

DeYoung, P. (2022) *Understanding and Treating Chronic Shame: Healing Right
Brain Relational Trauma*, 2nd edition, New York: Routledge.

Fisher, J. (2017) *Healing the Fragmented Selves of Trauma Survivors*, New York:
Routledge.

Herman, J. (2015) *Trauma and Recovery*, New York: Basic Books.

Thompson, B. (2008) *Counselling for Asperger Couples*, London: Jessica Kingsley.

PROFESSIONALISM

Sex therapy in the UK has been developing rapidly over the past few years so that more people are becoming aware of it, assisted by the media. Recently, there have been far more articles about sex and relationship issues, many including quotes from therapists, and there have been numerous reality and fictional television shows, radio programmes, films and podcasts which portray sex therapy in some form. At the same time, many people seem more motivated to explore or reclaim their sexuality, so therapy has seemed increasingly relevant to those who might not previously have considered it. They may go directly to a therapist or talk to a health professional they're already in contact with, such as a nurse, GP or support worker. We need to be aware that they could have developed expectations of the kind of support and therapy they'll receive based on media therapy, so clients may expect a lot from a single session.

PERSONAL DEVELOPMENT

It's often difficult to know whether to tell people about work as a sex therapist, as they can make erroneous assumptions about what it involves. Family, friends, clients, and even therapists working in other areas often tell us we must have heard some extraordinary stories and expect us to encounter the unusual and the exciting on a daily basis. Yet surprising presentations are rare. Most involve functional issues or performance anxiety and self-doubt; only once in a blue moon do we see anything out of the ordinary. Admittedly, our ordinary isn't everyone else's daily experience, but there's little that could be described as either comical or shocking. Yet sex therapists on television

DOI: 10.4324/9781003265641-7

and in the movies are usually portrayed as wacky and/or sex-obsessed. Moreover, any therapy involving an issue as personal and sensitive as sex needs to be treated with care and caution, especially as in some places and times sex 'therapy' has been offered by **sexual surrogates** or sex workers. Though this can be appropriate for some people, this is not currently part of mainstream sex therapy in the UK. However, on rare occasions we do meet clients who think sex therapy is a way of obtaining sex or couples who are afraid that sex therapy will involve performing sexual acts in the therapy room. So both therapists' and clients' personal safety and boundaries are important considerations, as is therapists' own mental health. It can be helpful to send out information about what sex therapy involves when receiving enquiries or to include such information on your website. A biography may also be helpful to demonstrate you have professional qualifications and experience. It's useful to ensure colleagues are aware of what sex therapy involves, so they can consult appropriately, make relevant referrals and explain something of the process to clients they refer.

IMAGE

The personal impact of taking on a sex therapy role can be surprising. It's sometimes necessary to educate colleagues about the work if they see it as less respected than, say, medical interventions or other forms of psychotherapy. Health professionals who've taken on sex education or therapy roles have also reported finding themselves differently positioned at work, as though they've revealed something intimate about themselves. Sex therapists' partners may feel they've been differently positioned too – as though they've now been publicly identified as sexually adventurous, for instance. Sometimes other family members can be embarrassed or feel they're expected to have more sexual knowledge and experience because of their association with us. Equally, others can be incredibly proud of the work we do, but few understand it until they've been sex therapy clients themselves.

EROTIC TRANSFERENCE

Transference is behaviour towards someone *as if* they were another person from their past. This can happen very easily in therapy, as little may be known about the therapist, providing a blank slate for them to create the practitioner they need. Sometimes clients treat the therapist as if they are their demanding and critical parent, for instance, or they may idealise them as a nurturing and protective carer. As many people have never before received the interest, attention or understanding therapy offers, it's understandable they would become attached to their therapist.

EROTIC TRANSFERENCE

In sex therapy, where the content is so personal, it becomes more likely that clients may eroticise the relationship and imagine themselves in sexual situations with their therapist. For most clients, this is either unconscious or they're aware that it's a fantasy.

Rarely, clients may believe a strong attraction is mutual and be disappointed or angry when the therapist doesn't follow through. This possibility terrifies many therapists who avoid signs of transference or end therapy if they think it's happening. Some work with the transference, even routinely expecting it, addressing the client's unmet needs and their management.

It goes without saying that therapists should not take advantage of their clients sexually or in any other way. It's unlikely that any therapist will get through their career without being attracted to a client, but this is for the therapist to manage with support from their supervisor if necessary. Both therapists' countertransference and clients' transference provides valuable information for the work, even when it isn't discussed between them. When it becomes overt, it makes sense to address it as soon as possible, demonstrating clear boundaries whilst acknowledging the client's needs and exploring how these can be met in the client's own life rather than in the therapy.

SELF-CARE

All therapists should feel safe in their work and may feel safer if they take some precautionary measures. For instance, you need detailed registration information for clients, with their full name, address, date of birth, contact and GP details in case these should be required for any reason, such as safeguarding issues. In agency settings there should ideally be a receptionist or chaperone outside the therapy rooms, and therapists may carry alarms. In private practice, it's safest to work from rooms on the ground floor facing the street. Clients' privacy is obviously important, but seating can often be arranged so that only the therapist's face can be seen from the road.

It's necessary to be clear and consistent about how clients should contact you and not to provide private phone numbers. Boundaries can also be set out in client agreements, explaining the payment procedure and penalties for cancellation. No-one should feel obliged to continue working with clients who overstep in ways that feel sexually predatory or unsafe.

Indemnity insurance is important in case of serious complaints or accidents. If clients are being seen in your home or office, you need to consider safety and accessibility.

It's also vital to manage caseloads so they're not top-heavy with difficulty. Ideally, sex therapists will have clients at different stages of the process and different degrees of trauma. We need events to look forward to, proper breaks, adequate rest, nutrition and sleep, as well as the ability to seek help when we need to. Some sex therapists assume they shouldn't be affected by their clients, but even the most straightforward and happy couples can be challenging.

Most of us have either had romantic or sexual relationships ourselves or witnessed them, particularly between our parents. It's therefore likely that our own material can be triggered by our clients' content, and we need to be able to recognise and manage this. Some training courses require students to undertake their own therapy to better enable them to spot and address their triggers and countertransference. Sex therapy isn't usually required, but it can be helpful to keep checking in with oneself to ensure any personal material that's been activated can be recognised and resulting needs met. Supervision and personal development groups can provide valuable support, allowing therapists to discuss their experiences. As the work is relevant to the entire life span and to multiple settings, it's important that therapists are able to share their knowledge and resources and to feel supported in the role itself.

SOCIAL MEDIA

It's increasingly difficult to remain completely private as clients can now search therapists' names online and potentially find out about other work, hobbies and activities. Therapists are also more active in the media, with professional forums, blogs, podcasts, live streams, websites or pages that solicit attention. These are a great way of sharing information and attracting clients, but it's important that personal media remains separate. In practice, it can be difficult to avoid some crossover, as other people may tag you in photographs or messages. Care is consequently needed about what's posted and your management of privacy settings. Though some therapists initially feel they don't mind what clients know, personal details can sometimes interfere with the therapeutic relationship. Couples struggling with infertility may be distressed by seeing their therapist's happy family photos, for instance, or may feel the therapist can't understand what they've been experiencing.

Clients often send friend requests or follow their therapists on social media. Though this is rarely a problem on professional accounts, it may be worth including a mention of what you will and won't respond to in your contracting and to give clear advice about the way to reach you. Some younger clients may routinely make contact via social media sites rather than texting or e-mailing, which is not much use if you rarely check your messages.

REFLEXIVITY

Reflexivity involves thinking about one's thinking. Often used in research to consider how the researcher influences the research process, reflexivity involves the consideration of how we reach conclusions and develop ideas, what influences the way we think and what this then means to us. If we were using processes of reflection, we would probably draw some conclusions from this consideration and plan some sort of response. However, though we may do this, reflexivity is about much more than reflection and self-awareness. These are the jumping off points for reflexivity, which produces meaning that also needs exploration. As everything leads to more questions and more meaning, it's likely this process will bring about some sort of change. After all, by the end of it, someone would be bound to know more than when they began. This knowledge will change the way they feel about themselves. Recognition of the effect of their process on their work and clients, and the mutual effect this then has on the therapist, creates a recursive process which is continuously developing. Reflexive thinking here involves a detailed internal process which creates connections, progressing between questions, exploration, and solutions. The therapist can now use this to deepen understanding and create more change if desired.

CAREER DEVELOPMENT

As sex therapy is a rapidly evolving area, sex therapists need to consider ways to maintain their personal and professional development. COSRT members receive the journal *Sexual and Relationship Therapy*, and membership of the British Society for Sexual Medicine (BSSM) includes a subscription to the *Journal of Sexual Medicine*. Since the pandemic, much more training has been available online and there have been more twilight events, as well as generally available podcasts plus radio and television programmes. Nevertheless, finding time to keep up with reading and courses can be challenging. It may help to make a rule that you'll read or catch up with self-access training when you have a free or cancelled session. It's also important to be aware of what's happening in the news, as stories about sex and relationships affecting celebrities or in soaps, dramas, documentaries and reality television can generate referrals.

Professional organisations can be helpful in keeping up with legal requirements and social changes that may be relevant to sex therapy practice. Both COSRT and the BSSM have useful information on their websites as well as offering training themselves. There's more about career progress in Chapter 1.

ETHICS

Members of the public who use the services of sex therapists are entitled to protection and adequate standards of competency and professionalism. Many UK sex therapists are members of COSRT which has its own code of ethics and practice and a register of practitioners and supervisors who follow the code, providing an extremely helpful framework. As well as offering practical guidance on day-to-day matters, it also asks practitioners to consider the unexpected. For instance, it tells us we must have someone to manage our clients if the work ends suddenly – usually due to serious illness or death – and how to raise concerns or deal with safety issues.

CONFIDENTIALITY

Therapists in private practice are required to comply with General Data Protection Regulations (GDPR) if any online material is stored or if there is online interaction, such as agreement to your website's cookies. Registration, for which there is an annual fee, implies that you're complying with the rules. These are basically about obtaining clients' consent for the way their details are used and for protecting their privacy. This extends to not sending out unsolicited mail to them and keeping files safely.

Clients are entitled to see their files if they wish. This may be more complicated with couples as both need to agree to them being shared. It's sensible to keep files brief and factual, focusing on your interventions rather than clients' pathology and personal information, and certainly not your opinions. History-taking files are normally shredded at the end of therapy, as a summary exists in the formulation and other personal information is no longer needed.

It's not just statutory regulations that may concern us. Sex and relationship work potentially presents therapists with ethical challenges, particularly when we find ourselves with information about one partner that the other isn't aware of. However, working with both partners often makes the situation much clearer than it can be when only one side of a story is available.

As information from the history taking sessions is discussed in formulation, it's important to be very clear about the boundaries of confidentiality. Normally, UK therapists would never share information from one partner's session with the other, so it's important to keep checking what's okay to share and what's private. Clients shouldn't be deterred from giving you helpful information because they fear their partner will find out. Sometimes, clients expect us to share information from individual sessions or to pass on messages to their partner that they don't wish to convey themselves, so it needs to be made clear that this isn't the therapist's role.

To help clients to feel comfortable that their material will remain private, it's important they're reassured you wouldn't break confidentiality unless there was a serious safeguarding issue that required you to do so; even then, in many cases clients would be informed. They do need to be aware of any circumstances where their case may be discussed, such as in supervision or in a case study or research. Many therapists have consent forms to cover all such possibilities which clients are asked to sign at the beginning of therapy. Later on, they may worry about damaging the rapport with their therapist if they refuse.

CONSENT

We need to obtain clients' consent if we're going to show them any explicit material, including diagrams of genitals. It's also helpful to agree that it's okay for either partner to organise a private session with the therapist if they need it. It's often useful for someone to explore ways of talking to their partner about sensitive issues, new thoughts that are bothering them, changes to the relationship which aren't being aired or undeclared personal information that they now wish to share. It's also much safer for a client to reveal abuse if private sessions have been discussed in this way at the outset.

Consent between the couple also requires our attention. When there's loss of desire, we need to be certain that both partners really do wish to be sexual together. This is one of the most common ethical issues in sex therapy, as a partner will often say they wish to be sexual to please the other when this isn't the case. It may be that they do wish they enjoyed sex but they never have and find it an ordeal. Sometimes a partner has threatened to leave if the other doesn't comply, which puts the therapy under too much pressure to be successful. Therapists shouldn't be put in a position of colluding with this, though they can be helpful in exploring ways to manage the extent of the non-sexual partner's sexual behaviour or what alternatives may be acceptable to them.

WORKING ONLINE

Since the coronavirus pandemic, more sex therapy has been conducted online, which many clients have appreciated as it means they avoid travel and babysitting costs. However, there can be challenges to privacy if clients are afraid of being overheard by others in the house. Clear boundaries may be needed around what's acceptable during a session, as clients can feel the context is much more casual than they would expect in face-to-face appointments. Before arranging online sessions, consider how you feel about clients in pyjamas, or even in bed, and how you'll deal with issues like clients eating, smoking or drinking alcohol during a call.

On the whole, clients are in their own homes and it's obviously inappropriate to tell them how they're allowed to behave. However, it's helpful to offer guidelines around what works best in your contract with them. For example, use of alcohol or substances before or during a session isn't ethical if it means you're working with someone whose thinking may be affected or who may not remember what was discussed.

Pets and babies in the room can be distracting and they may become upset if there are moments of tension or distress. Though it should be expected, an environment that's quiet, private, and comfortable isn't always possible, and we may gain insight into our clients' lives in unexpected ways. Similarly, online working may give clients more insight into their therapists' lives if they can see their homes. Ideally, you'll have a neutral or blurred background if the platform allows this and avoid family photographs or items which give information about your similarity or difference to the clients. Therapists also need to consider their own privacy and noise levels.

You need to be reasonably competent with technology, ensure you're working with an encrypted video platform and that you have up-to-date, functioning firewalls and virus protection. Clients may need advice ahead of sessions about the security of their own devices. Not all browsers work with all video platforms either, so clients may need advice about downloading alternatives. You also need to be clear in your contract about the procedure if there is an internet or power failure.

When conducting therapy with clients abroad, it's wise to state in your contracts that you'll be working to the laws of the country in which you reside. Check your insurance cover accords with this, as problems could still develop in countries where therapy practitioners require a medical qualification. This particularly applies to

North America, but elsewhere as well. COSRT advises that online practitioners have carried out such research and should be clinically experienced, with supervisors who are also experienced in online working. This may become relevant if your competence comes into question for any reason, such as a complaint.

A serious concern for therapists is what happens if a call ends suddenly or if a client is distressed, suicidal, or appears at risk when a session ends. While we may be able to manage client safety in an office setting, it's much more difficult when they're remote. It can be helpful to obtain details of a supportive friend or family member at the outset of therapy, with agreement that these are for emergency use if you are sufficiently concerned. It may sometimes be necessary to carry out welfare calls or messaging outside of sessions to check on safety and wellbeing if you're concerned about a client. Be clear in your contracting that confidentiality will be broken if you're sufficiently worried, so that you can contact the GP or emergency services if necessary. It's also important clients know how to contact you, both in an emergency and in order to make changes to an appointment.

SUPERVISION

Adequate supervision is essential for ethical practice. It's easy to overlook safeguarding concerns and potential insights when we're very involved with a case or when it resonates with our own material, or we can find ourselves taking sides or losing curiosity and interest. As we gain experience, we begin to discover how much more there is to learn. Indeed, we can never stop learning, as the discipline progresses and our practice changes us. Much of sex therapy practice is also counterintuitive, such as asking clients *not* to discuss their sensate focus experiments, and disproves much of what we're told in popular media. An experienced supervisor should provide enabling, nonjudgemental space for a practitioner's learning journey to unfurl. Practitioners can assist this process by being prepared for supervision, with an awareness of what they want from each session. Supervision shouldn't be about pleasing the supervisor or proving what you can do, but could be about looking for what will support you best. This may develop over time, so it's helpful to occasionally review together what is working and what could change.

CHAPTER SUMMARY

- The role of sex therapists is often misunderstood.
- Sex therapists have professional responsibilities to their clients and themselves to engage in safe practice, following statutory and professional guidelines.

FURTHER READING

BACP (2019) *Working Online in the Counselling Professions*, Lutterworth: BACP.

Benns, J., Burridge, S. & Penman, J. (2021) *Intimacy, Sex and Relationship Challenges Laid Bare Across the Lifespan: Applied Principles and Practice for Health Professionals*, Abingdon: Routledge.

Wadley, J.C. & Siegel, R. [eds] (2019) *The Art of Sex Therapy Supervision*, New York: Routledge.

RESOURCES

British Society for Sexual Medicine: bssm.org.uk.

COSRT Good Therapy Code of Ethics and Practice 2019: www.cosrt.org.uk/wp-content/uploads/2019/11/Good-Therapy-COSRT-Code-of-Ethics-and-Practice-2019-1.pdf.

COSRT Practice Guideline 9: *Online Therapy and Supervision*. www.cosrt.org.uk/wp-content/uploads/2018/12/Doc-15.-Practice-Guideline-9.-Online-Therapy-and-Supervision-18.08.16-HH-amends-v2.pdf.

GDPR Registration: https://ico.org.uk/for-organisations/data-protection-fee/self-assessment/.

BIBLIOGRAPHY

Ladson, D. & Welton, R. (2007) Recognizing and managing erotic and eroticized transferences, *Psychiatry (Edgmont)*, 4(4), 47–50.

GLOSSARY

BDSM	Bondage, discipline/dominance, submission/sadism and masochism.
Cisgender	Description of someone who identifies with the gender assigned to them at birth.
Compersion	Joy in seeing a partner happy with someone else.
Dildo	Sex toy shaped like a penis.
Discourse	Beliefs, thinking and behaviour relating to a particular subject.
Dissociation	Unconscious reaction to traumatic or unwanted thoughts, feelings or situations whereby someone withdraws or becomes taken over by a management strategy (part). As a result, trauma remains unprocessed.
Double bind	A situation where two messages conflict, and choosing either or neither will create problems.
Edging	Repeatedly ceasing sexual arousal just before ejaculation, which can lead to more intense and prolonged orgasm.
EMDR	Eye Movement Desensitisation and Reprocessing, a technique using rapid eye movement and/or rhythm which takes the emotion out of painful memories, and so works especially well to treat trauma.

DOI: 10.4324/9781003265641-8

Endometriosis   Condition in which tissue similar to the uterus (womb) lining occurs in other areas outside the uterus, causing pain during menstruation.

Fantasy bond   Belief that a relationship has qualities and attachment that don't actually exist.

Heteronormative   Idea that binary performance of gender and heterosexuality is natural and superior.

Incels   Mainly online subculture of 'involuntarily celibate' men who blame 'masculine' men and the women who are attracted to them for their own inability to find a sexual partner.

Internalized homophobia   Shame associated with minority oppression.

Labiaplasty   Surgery on the female genitals, sometimes to treat intersex conditions, but mostly to improve the appearance of the labia minora.

Latency period   Time between the onset of sexual stimulation and ejaculation.

Leathermen   A gay masculine subculture which eroticises leather, often alongside interests in motorcycles and BDSM.

Masters and Johnson   Sex researchers who studied human sexual response and developed sex therapy based on CBT.

Mentalization   The ability to think about one's own thinking and to wonder about the thinking of others; an ability to go beyond binary thinking and use curiosity to avoid assumptions.

Neuropathy   Disease of peripheral nerves far from the brain and spinal cord, which can cause alteration or loss of sensation.

Opening up   The process of becoming polyamorous.

Ovulation   Release of an egg from the ovary.

Parts therapies   Exploration of different personality parts to explain personal conflict, understand motivation and gain more personal control.

PDE 5 inhibitors   Vasodilating drugs, such as Viagra, which facilitate erection when accompanied by sexual stimulation.

Pegging	Anal penetration with a strap-on, often by women to men.
Phallocentric	Concerned with the penis.
PiV sex	Penis-in-vagina sex.
Point of inevitability	Extreme sexual arousal, beyond which ejaculation becomes inevitable.
Refractory period	Time following orgasm before a further erection or orgasm can occur.
Sexual surrogates	Stand-in for partners in sex therapy. Introduced by Masters and Johnson, surrogates were most popular in the US in the 1980s, but this is not a recognised form of sex therapy in the UK.
Simmering	Exercise which allows the repeated gradual build up and release of sexual tension or arousal in men, which may result in a more intense eventual orgasm.
Strap-on	Dildo which straps onto the body, allowing people with no penis to penetrate.
Surgical menopause	Occurs when the ovaries are removed by operation, causing a sudden withdrawal of oestrogen, rather than menopause occurring gradually as oestrogen reduces naturally.
Swinging	Partner swapping.
Systemic therapy	Rather than just exploring the behaviour and thinking of an individual, systemic therapy's focus is relational, looking at the dynamics of an entire system. This could be a couple, nuclear family, extended family, other organisations they belong to, and even wider society/culture.
Top surgery	Mastectomy and chest contouring surgery carried out for trans men.
Vaginismus	Inability to have PiV sex due to involuntary tightening of the pelvic floor muscles.
Vanilla sex	Now unpopular term which may be used to describe non-kinky sex.

INDEX

Printed in the United States
by Baker & Taylor Publisher Services